DO NOT REMOVE
CARDS FROM POCKET

Campaign
Financing

CAMPAIGN FINANCING

*Politics
and the
Power
of Money*

Suzanne M. Coil

*The Millbrook Press
Brookfield, Connecticut*

Issue and Debate

To my editor, Elaine Pascoe, for her wisdom and understanding, to Judie Mills for her kindness, and to Karen Bornemann Spies for her professional help, I gratefully offer my sincere appreciation and thanks.

SMC

Photographs courtesy of UPI/Bettmann: pp. 11, 14, 46; AP/Wide World Photos: pp. 22, 73, 78, 84; © Brad Markel, Gamma-Liaison: p. 29; The Granger Collection: p. 35; The Bettmann Archive: pp. 38, 40; Rothco Cartoons: pp. 53, 89; © Jose R. Lopez, The New York Times Inc.: p. 64; Reuters/Bettmann: p. 68.

Library of Congress Cataloging-in-Publication Data

Coil, Suzanne M.
Campaign financing : politics and the power of money / Suzanne M. Coil.
p.   cm.—(Issue and debate)
Includes bibliographical references and index.
ISBN 1-56294-220-4 (lib. bdg.)
1. Campaign funds—United States—Juvenile literature.
[1. Campaign funds. 2. Elections. 3. Politics, Practical.]
I. Title. II. Series.
JK1991.C637   1994
324.7'8'0973—dc20   93-8716   CIP   AC

Published by The Millbrook Press
2 Old New Milford Road, Brookfield, Connecticut 06804

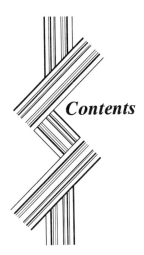

Contents

Also by Suzanne M. Coil

Florida

George Washington Carver

Harriet Beecher Stowe

Mardi Gras!

Poisonous Plants

The Poor in America

Robert Hutchings Goddard:
Pioneer of Rocketry and Space Flight

For Jesse
who knows the difference between
"going somewhere" and "just traveling"

The Campaign Money Crisis

The United States prides itself on its system of representative government and its free economy. The principle of "one person, one vote" protects the rights of citizens to take part in the political process, and the U.S. economic system affords individuals the opportunities they need to prosper. Yet, as proud as Americans are of their system, few are not aware that the country faces massive problems—in health care, education, the environment, transportation, housing, employment, soaring federal budget deficits, crime, and poverty. Politicians talk endlessly about these problems, but little is done to solve them. And Americans feel increasingly disillusioned about the political process. Many no longer bother to vote; even in presidential elections, only about half of eligible voters typically turn out.

Lack of information about issues and candidates, cumbersome voter registration procedures, disgust with negative campaigns, dissatisfaction with the procedures by which candidates are selected—all these factors are frequently blamed for voter apathy. Most important, however, is the fact that many people feel their votes count for little in elections that are increasingly dominated by the power of money. Money—specifically, the funds that politicians raise to run campaigns and win elections—has corrupted the political process, they believe. Through a system that encourages huge contributions and massive campaign spending, wealthy individuals and special interest groups gain access to and, some people charge, control of the politicians who run government.

Concern about this issue led President Bill Clinton to propose a campaign-finance reform plan during his first months in office. The Clinton plan, announced in May 1993, offered public subsidies to congressional candidates who agreed to limit campaign spending, and it sought to lessen the influence of lobbyists and others who represent special interests by restricting their campaign contributions. Even before it was officially announced, however, the proposal prompted sharp debate. Republican congressional leaders asserted that the plan was designed to keep Democrats in office, and they vowed to defeat it. Others said the plan did not go far enough to end the corrupting influence of money on national politics.

Clinton's plan was not the first attempt to reform campaign financing, and as the debate continued it was clear that it would not be the last. Concern about the role of money in politics goes back to the beginning of the United States. However, reform efforts have been growing since the 1960s and 1970s, when a series of events focused national attention on the problem.

Kennedy's Commission. When John F. Kennedy ran for president in 1960, his opponents charged that his family wealth gave him an unfair advantage in the race. They accused the Kennedys of spending vast amounts of money in an attempt to buy the election. At a political dinner, JFK

John F. Kennedy campaigns in 1960. After
he took office as president in 1961,
Kennedy appointed a bipartisan commission
to study campaign financing reform.

answered these charges with humor. He read a fake telegram, supposedly sent by his father, Joseph P. Kennedy. "Don't buy one vote more than necessary," the message said. "I'll be damned if I'll pay for a landslide."[1]

Once in office, however, Kennedy expressed concern that eventually only the rich would be able to run for office. Alarmed at the rising cost of election campaigns, he named a bipartisan commission to study the idea of having the U.S. government pay the cost of presidential campaigns. This was the beginning of an election reform movement that blossomed in the early 1970s.

Reform focused on regulating ways in which money was raised and spent in political campaigns. In 1971, Congress passed the Federal Election Campaign Act (FECA), a landmark law designed to overhaul campaign financing. For the first time, the law set limits on the amount that federal candidates could spend on media advertising and required candidates to fully disclose campaign contributions and expenditures. It was set to take effect on April 7, 1972.

The Watergate Scandal. Before this, some candidates had collected secret campaign contributions totaling millions of dollars—well over limits set by previous legislation. However, this legislation had rarely been enforced. Knowing that the opportunity for secret money-raising would soon end, many politicians increased their efforts to collect campaign contributions before the deadline. Among them was President Richard M. Nixon.

Some of these contributions were used to finance a break-in at the Watergate offices of the Democratic National Committee in Washington. Seven men who worked for the Committee to Re-elect the President (CREEP) stole important papers and planted electronic listening devices in an effort to try to learn information about the Democratic party campaign.

Perhaps the break-in and the illegal contributions would have remained a secret had it not been for the actions of a citizen group, Common Cause. In September 1972, Common Cause sued CREEP for failure to report election contributions made before April 7 of that year. By forcing the disclosure of secret contributions to Nixon's campaign, Common Cause helped open the door to investigations that uncovered the illegal and criminal activities that came to be known as the Watergate scandal.

Altogether, nearly $20 million in unreported funds had been raised by the Nixon camp before the April 7 deadline. Of that total, $1.5 million had been collected in cash. The investigation revealed a substantial number of illegal corporate donations. The dairy industry alone had pledged $2 million to Nixon's campaign. Herbert Kalmbach, who had headed the corporate gifts operation, pleaded guilty to illegal campaign practices. He was fined $10,000 and sentenced to prison.

The Nixon campaign had also collected sizable contributions from individuals. W. Clement Stone, a Chicago insurance executive, had donated $2 million. Richard Scaife, heir to an immense banking and oil fortune, had donated $1 million. The multimillionaire Howard Hughes had given $100,000 in cash, which was stashed in a safe-deposit box.

According to John W. Gardner, who was chairman of Common Cause at the time, the Watergate affair was not primarily a tale of political espionage or White House intrigue. Rather, it was a terrible chapter in the history of campaign financing, since the funds paid to the Watergate conspirators before and after the break-in came from campaign gifts.

President Richard M. Nixon announces his resignation in 1974. The disclosure of secret contributions to his 1972 campaign helped uncover the Watergate scandal.

Gardner's assertion was confirmed when, on August 5, 1974, President Nixon released the tape recording of a conversation he'd had in June 1972 with H. R. Haldeman, then White House chief of staff. The tape revealed that Nixon knew the Watergate break-in had been financed with campaign funds and that he had agreed to help in the illegal cover-up. Four days later, on August 9, 1974, Nixon resigned from office.

The disclosures of widespread abuses in campaign financing in the Watergate scandal fueled a far-reaching congressional debate. Campaign finance reform legislation enacted by Congress following the Watergate scandal included special provisions to control and monitor campaign contributions by individuals. To prevent wealthy individuals from dominating campaigns and controlling candidates, the new legislation stated that an individual could contribute no more than $1,000 to a federal candidate for each election, counting the primary, general election, and runoff (should there be one) as three separate elections. Furthermore, individuals were prohibited from donating more than $25,000 combined to all federal candidates in a single year.

The Scope of the Problem. Despite this legislation, campaign costs continued to grow. In 1980 congressional candidates spent $239 million on their election campaigns. By 1988 this figure had risen to $459 million. Four years later the total had soared to $678 million, an increase of 52 percent over the amount spent in 1990.[2]

These figures point out a crucial factor in today's system of free elections: money. According to Herbert Alexander, director of the Citizens' Research Foundation:

- The voting population is growing, occupying urban, suburban, and rural areas. The rapid development of communications media, especially television, makes it easier but far more costly to run political campaigns.

- In some states, a Senate campaign may cost more than ten times the salary paid to the winner during his or her term of office.

- The yearly budgets of the Republican National Committee and the Democratic National Committee run to millions of dollars, even in non-election years. This is the size of the budget of a small business corporation.[3]

Many elected officials and those who study government are concerned about the relationship between money and our political process. Writing in the late 1980s, political writer Elizabeth Drew commented:

The role that money is currently playing in American politics is different both in scope and in nature from anything that has gone before. The acquisition of campaign funds has become an obsession on the part of nearly every candidate for federal office. The obsession leads the candidates to solicit and accept money from those most able to provide it, and to adjust their behavior in office to the need for money—and the fear that a challenger might be able to obtain more.[4]

Senator Robert Byrd agreed:

I know something about how Senators have to go out and spend their time in this grubby, demeaning task of trying to raise money for the re-election campaigns. They are forced to do it by necessity.

They are simply facing up to the realities of the era in which we live, the electronic age—computers, media consultants, expensive mailing lists, all of these things. But they have to do it. It is a case of survival. Self-survival is one of the first laws of nature and they are being forced to engage in this unceasing, ever-increasing demand for money, money, money—the money chase.

I am concerned that if something is not done about it, we are going to see things go from bad to worse, and the faith and confidence and trust that the people should accord to this institution, the legislative branch, are going to be undermined.[5]

Bribery or Democracy? The key question regarding the role of money in election campaigns is whether or not it has distorted the process by which our elected officials are supposed to function. Are campaign contributions a way to buy influence with a politician, or are they a form of participation in the political process?

One viewpoint is that private campaign contributions are a way for special interests to influence the policies and decisions of elected officials, since candidates may feel pressured to make policy choices in favor of those who have contributed to their campaigns. Once elected, these officials may be more concerned about raising money for re-election than about how their policies and decisions will affect voters.

An opposing viewpoint is held by those who believe that contributions to campaigns are a way to participate in the democratic process. They believe that the act of writing a check in support of a candidate is an expression of free speech—in short, democracy in action. They are opposed to limiting campaign contributions, contending that campaign spending does not overly influence officials. There are a wide variety of interest groups competing for the attention of each elected official, they contend, so officials will be able to achieve compromises between conflicting demands and won't be controlled by just one interest group.

Our system of government is based on the principle of "one person, one vote." In other words, each citizen should have an equal opportunity to serve in public office and take part in the political process. Unfortunately, not all citizens have access to the same economic resources. How are the differences in resources to be handled? Should all candidates be given an equal amount of money to use in their campaigns? If so, where is the money to come from?

This book will discuss these questions. It will show how money affects the decisions made by our lawmakers, how money from small special-interest groups affects representative government in the United States, and how our system of campaign finance costs voters and consumers billions of dollars every year. In the chapters that follow, we will explore the process of campaign financing, and the political, social, and ethical questions it raises. We will also examine the history of campaign financing in the United States and tackle some sticky questions. Just how much money do politicians need to run their campaigns? Why is the cost of running for office so high? How do politicians raise the money? Do politicians favor the interests of wealthy contributors over the interests of their poorer constituents? Can political costs be reduced without damage to our democratic system? Finally, we will discuss current proposals for reform of the system. Is there a better way? If so, what is it?

2

On the Campaign Money Trail

Imagine that you're fed up with the mess in Washington. You think you could do a better job yourself, so you decide to run for public office. You might decide that you want to represent your congressional district in the House of Representatives. Or you might want to become one of the two senators who represent your state in the Senate. Someday, you might even choose to run for president of the United States. You're young, creative, and idealistic. You've studied all the issues, your head is full of new ideas, and you're not afraid of hard work. If you're elected, you'll fight to change things for the better. You're convinced you can make a difference.

Your opponent, Horatio Fuzzbottle, has been in office for many years. His campaign speeches are full of promises he doesn't keep. He doesn't answer phone calls and letters from his constituents, he never seems to be around when needed, and there are rumors that he's not exactly honest. Yet, every time he comes up for re-election, Fuzzbottle wins. You're sure the reason voters keep sending him back to Washington is that he's never faced a real challenger. In other words, he's never had to campaign against you.

You know that people in your community are enthusiastic about your ideas. Everyone seems eager for a change, and your friends are urging you to place your name on the ballot for the next election. It should be easy to defeat Mr. Fuzzbottle, right? Wrong!

Before you enter the political arena, you would do well to heed the words of former House Speaker Thomas "Tip" O'Neill, who advised that there are four parts to any campaign: the candidate, the issues of the candidate, the campaign organization, and the money for running the campaign. Without money, however, O'Neill said, "You can forget the other three."

So, like all challengers, you have a hard fight ahead of you. You will have to run two campaigns—a political campaign and a fund-raising campaign—and you must excel in both campaigns if you are to win. You may be better qualified than your opponent, your ideas may have more appeal to voters, your campaign organization may be staffed with enthusiastic professionals and volunteers, and your ideals and ethics may shine like gold, but unless you are able to raise more money than Mr. Fuzzbottle can raise, you are almost certainly doomed to failure.

Three Key Factors. In planning your fund-raising campaign, you will have to take into account three important developments that have changed the American political scene since the 1970s. First, because of the election laws mentioned in Chapter 1, you won't be able to accept contributions of more than $2,000 from any single individual. This means you can't rely on a few "fat cats" for money. If you are wealthy, you may give an unlimited amount of money to your own campaign. But if you're like most politicians, you will have to cultivate many other sources for campaign funds.

The second development you must consider is the dramatic change in the way political campaigns are conducted. Well into the twentieth century, politicians were able to get their messages across by traveling from town to town, giving speeches at chicken dinners and barbecues. Politicians no longer follow the chicken dinner route if they wish to be elected. Everything changed with the advent of television and, later, the computer. Today's successful political campaigns are elaborate hi-tech affairs, involving polls, consultants, direct mail, television advertising, telephone solicitations, and scores of other specialized techniques.

As campaigns have increased in sophistication, they have also become more costly. In fact, beginning in the 1970s the costs of running for public office have skyrocketed. According to the Federal Election Commission, spending for all candidates for the House of Representatives was $407 million in 1992, up 53 percent from 1990. A total of $270.3 million was spent in 1992 Senate contests, compared with $180.4 million in the 1990 races. However, this included two elections in California that by themselves accounted for $34 million in expenditures.[1]

Presidential campaigns are even more expensive. In 1972 the presidential candidates spent a combined total of $137.8 million. According to the *Congressional Quarterly*, George Bush and Bill Clinton, 1992 presidential candidates for the Republican and Democratic parties respectively, spent $80 million in "soft money"—contributions to political parties from individual and corporate donors, which fall outside limits on direct donations to federal candidates. Some of these donations were as much as $100,000 each.[2] In addition, the Federal Election Commission gave each

Texas businessman H. Ross Perot campaigns in 1992. The independent candidate spent millions of dollars of his own funds in an effort to win the presidency.

party nominee $55.24 million in federal matching funds, while their political parties received over $11 million each in matching funds.[3] Millionaire Ross Perot, who campaigned as an independent, did not accept federal matching and was therefore allowed to spend as much of his private funds as he wished.

The third factor, one that will affect you greatly, is the growth of political action committees (PACs). Simply put, PACs are groups of people who pool their money in order to contribute it to candidates who share their views. Because PACs can, and do, give large amounts of money to favored candidates, their growth and influence have changed the face of politics. The power of PACs, and the role they play in the political process, will be discussed in detail in Chapter 4.

As in any race, there are winners and losers. Of course, you want to win. So just how much money will you need to wage a successful campaign? A review of recent spending patterns will give you some idea. In the 1992 elections the 435 candidates elected to the House of Representatives spent an average of about $551,000 each in their campaigns. This is a sharp increase from the average of $412,000 spent by winners in 1990. House challengers spent an average of $83,201 if they were Republican, triple the figure of two years prior. Democratic challengers spent $68,324, double the 1990 spending levels.[4]

The costs of Senate races are more difficult to compare, since one-third of the Senate is elected every two years and total spending depends on which states are holding elections. Successful Senate campaigns average $4 million. In 1992 a total of $124.3 million was spent on winning Senate races, compared with the $115.4 million spent in 1990.[5]

All this talk of money is alarming. You ask, "Is all that money really necessary to win?" The answer is yes! The dollars you collect will be translated into communications designed to inform, influence, and motivate voters. Unless you are able to effectively get your message across to voters, you stand little chance of being elected.

Do you need to spend more money than your opponent, Mr. Fuzzbottle? Again, the answer is yes. In order to win, challengers nearly always must outspend incumbents. Incumbents in 1992 spent whatever they felt was necessary to maintain their leads over challengers. House incumbents involved in the most closely contested races, for example, spent an average of $788,000 each.[6]

While it is true that challengers with smaller campaign budgets sometimes win against incumbents, they are the exceptions, not the rule. When they do win, their success is usually due to some outside factor. For example, the incumbent might be involved in a scandal. Or, the incumbent might not take the challenger seriously and do little to ensure re-election. Another factor might be unusually low voter turnout on election day because of bad weather or voter apathy. Then again, the incumbent might be disabled by illness, thus leaving the field open for the challenger. The challenger might even be swept into office by riding on the "coattails" of a popular presidential candidate.

What are your chances of winning due to one of these factors? According to political consultant S. J. Guzzetta, they're not very good, since about 85 percent of all incumbents win re-election. Those who lose are typically defeated by a well-financed and professionally run campaign. In any given year, fewer than ten win as a result of an "outside" factor. Guzzetta concluded that it is foolish to run an underfinanced campaign with the hope that you'll have a stroke of luck.

Why will you need more money than your opponent? Because, like all incumbents, Mr. Fuzzbottle starts out with several distinct advantages. First of all, as a member of

Congress, he has a franking privilege, which means that he pays no postage on mail sent to his constituents. According to the National Taxpayers Union (a group of private citizens that keeps an eye on federal spending), members of Congress went on a "franking frenzy" during 1991, spending nearly $45 million of taxpayers' money on postage. With the congressional free-mail budget for the 1992 election year set at a staggering $80 million, it's easy to see why free postage offers your opponent a considerable advantage. You, of course, will have to pay for every postage stamp you use.

A second advantage your opponent has is that he can use his congressional staff to assist in his campaign. Their salaries, which are paid with tax dollars, are worth an additional $150,000 to $200,000 or more. You, on the other hand, will have to hire campaign workers and pay their salaries yourself.

Third, as incumbent, your opponent is well known in your district; his name, his face, and his positions on many issues are already familiar to thousands of voters. Because he is an elected official, his statements and routine appearances are reported by television, magazine, and newspaper reporters. He is interviewed frequently and is invited to appear on news programs and talk shows. This media coverage can be worth thousands of dollars, but your opponent won't have to pay for any of it. To make your name and face equally familiar to voters, you will have to pay for television and print media advertising. Later, after you have established yourself as a serious candidate, you will also be considered "news," but keeping your name and face before the voters will still require heavy spending.

Taking these advantages into consideration, it is easy to see why your opponent is way ahead of you before the campaign begins and any money is spent. By adding the value of the franking privilege and the benefit of using his congressional staff to work on his campaign, you can see that he is kicking off his campaign with hundreds of thousands of dollars of taxpayers' money at his disposal. That is why spending just as much as your opponent will not get you elected. To overcome his head start, you will need to spend more. And, in order to spend more, you'll need to raise much more money than he does.

But having a larger campaign chest than your opponent does not automatically guarantee that you will win. How effectively you spend the money is equally important. Like most politicians, you will seek the advice and services of professional political consultants, fund raisers, pollsters, and strategists. These hired specialists will help you develop a winning political strategy as well as a campaign to raise the funds to carry it through.

How will the money be spent? First of all, you must pay for the services of specialists. Because they are experts, they command large fees and commissions. But short of a miracle, you cannot expect to win without their help. Next, you will need to rent a campaign headquarters and pay for utilities, telephones, desks, typewriters, computers, file cabinets, campaign stationery, postage, and other office equipment and supplies. Although you have a corps of enthusiastic volunteers who will do such chores as stuffing envelopes, manning phone banks, and distributing campaign literature, you will still need to hire a dependable office staff.

You will spend lots of money on such items as bumper stickers, buttons, signs, balloons, and billboards. You will need hundreds of thousands of brochures and other direct-mail pieces, and you will pay writers, artists, typographers, and printers to produce them. Of course, you will also pay tens of thousands of dollars to mail these items.

You will find yourself spending a good deal of money on airline tickets, rented cars, and hotels as you travel around giving speeches, meeting voters, and attending dinners, rallies, and other fund-raising events. In the course of your campaign, you will discover that a significant amount of your time, effort, and money will be expended in the pursuit of campaign funds.

The price tag for all the activities and items mentioned can easily amount to hundreds of thousands—even millions—of dollars. Nevertheless, it does not include the price of television and radio advertising, the most costly item in your campaign budget. Depending on where you live, and how intensive a campaign you plan to run, your media expenses can equal or exceed your outlay for all other campaign activities combined. For example, North Carolina's Senator Jesse Helms spent a whopping $13.4 million on his 1990 re-election campaign—$9.7 million of which went for television advertising alone.

Changing Campaigns. During the first 150 years of our country's history, most citizens learned about federal candidates through newspapers, pamphlets, and other printed material. Then, with the invention of radio, politicians found a new way of campaigning. Radio was first used in the 1924 election when the Republican party opened its own radio stations on the East Coast.

President Franklin D. Roosevelt, however, was the first politician to realize the full potential of the new electronic medium. During World War II, millions of Americans gathered around their radios to hear the president's popular "fireside chats." Roosevelt's inspiring messages and reassuring voice made people feel confident and close to the man who was leading the country through difficult times.

After the war, Americans began buying television sets, and electronic campaigning (television and radio) began to play an important role in educating voters. Today, according to A. C. Nielsen, a consumer survey group, 98 percent of all American households have at least one television set.[7] Nearly half the households have two or more sets. In fact, there are more televisions in the United States than telephones, bathtubs, and flushing toilets.[8] Television has become the dominant political medium today.

As such, television accounts for an increasingly greater portion of campaign budgets. According to the Citizens' Research Foundation, overall spending in all political campaigns during the presidential election year of 1956 amounted to $155 million. Only $9.8 million of this total was spent on television and radio advertising. By 1968, overall campaign spending had doubled to $300 million, but candidates had increased their spending for television and radio advertising to $58.9 million, nearly six times the amount spent twelve years before. Like most successful politicians, you will spend a major portion of your campaign funds on television advertising.

The Money Chase. Where will the money come from? If you are a multimillionaire, like independent presidential candidate Ross Perot in 1992, you can bankroll your own campaign and not be bothered with the onerous task of fund-raising. However, if you are a candidate for president or vice president and you plan to accept public matching funds, you may spend no more than $50,000 of your own or your family's money on your campaign. Like most politicians, you will rely on three basic sources for campaign contributions: individual contributors, political parties, and special-interest groups.

If you rely on donations from individuals to amass the funds you need to run a successful campaign, you will need to solicit donations from thousands of people. To woo these potential donors, you will make phone calls, write letters, give speeches, attend dinners, shake hands, and

Bill and Hillary Clinton attend a Democratic fund-raising event soon after the 1992 election. The pursuit of campaign funds takes up a large part of most politicians' time.

even kiss a few babies. Since it is unlikely that you will find enough individuals willing to donate $1,000 to both your primary and general election campaigns, you will have to cultivate other sources for funds.

If you are a member of a major political party, you can ask your party for a contribution to your campaign. Party money can be given in two ways—as a "direct" contribution or as a "coordinated" expenditure. Direct contributions are funds given by the party to candidates to do with as they please. Current law allows each of the national party committees to give Senate candidates a total of $17,500 each during the year in which they are seeking election. A House candidate can receive a total of $10,000.

Coordinated spending, on the other hand, makes the party a partner in your campaign. Coordinated expenditures are made for such services as polling and television advertising production, but the party has a say in how the money is spent. The ceilings for coordinated spending, which are based on the voting age population and therefore vary from district to district and state to state, are much higher than those for direct giving. But in accepting "coordinated" funds, you must remember that the party has a say in how the money is spent. To avoid having the party tell you how to run your campaign, you may decide to appeal to this source of funding only if necessary.

If you are like most politicians, you will look to PACs to fund a major portion of your campaign. Current law allows a PAC to contribute $5,000 to a federal candidate for each election—that is, $5,000 for the primary and another $5,000 for the general election. PACs pour millions of dollars into federal elections, but most of the money is donated to incumbents. Although you're a challenger, don't be discouraged. There are nearly 5,000 PACs in the United States today, so chances are that a few are willing to donate money to your campaign. They may do so because they approve of your position on issues that are important to them, or they may contribute to your campaign because they want to see your opponent defeated.

Before you accept any PAC contributions, however, it would be wise to reflect on the old saying, "There is no such thing as a free lunch." When PACs give money to a candidate, they usually expect something in return. At a minimum, they will expect you to represent their interests fairly when you vote on legislation that may affect them. Be aware that when you accept PAC money, your critics may charge that you are being "bought" by special interests. The power of PACs and their controversial role in the political process will be discussed in depth later on.

For now, imagine that you have managed to amass the money you need. With the help of your consultants and volunteers, you have run an effective campaign. Finally, election day arrives. The ballots are counted. Congratulations! You are the winner!

The campaign was tiring, and you're glad it's over. As you look back at the past year, you realize that more than half of your time was spent raising money. Now that you've been elected, you're eager to get to work serving the people of your district as their representative in Congress for the next two years.

But wait. The campaign isn't over. Your campaign manager tells you that if you want to run for re-election in two years, you will have to begin, right now, to raise campaign funds. In fact, you may have to spend most of your time and attention raising money—as much as $4,000 every week for the next two years. If you had been elected to the Senate, you would have to raise more than $12,500 per week, every week for the next six years, if you plan to seek re-election.

To raise money for your next campaign, you will have to please the individuals and PACs who contributed in the past. Not only will they expect you to vote "their" way on issues, they will also expect you to answer their letters and phone calls, and to greet them when they visit your office.

The activities associated with fund-raising will leave you little time to respond to the requests of ordinary voters in your district. Nor will they allow you enough time to make a thorough study of the bewildering array of issues and legislation that confronts you as a member of Congress.

You are still full of idealism and good ideas, but you're beginning to feel discouraged. How will you find the time to do an effective job? How will you be able to fairly represent all the voters in your district? How, indeed, did the system get to be such a mess?

3
The History
of Campaign
Finance Reform

The more complex and costly political campaigns become, the more the democratic principle of political equality is threatened. It is easy therefore to understand why many American voters feel that their concerns are being ignored in favor of moneyed interests and that the power of money has distorted the electoral process. Their fears, however, are far from new.

Since colonial times, the problems connected with obtaining and spending campaign funds have worried politicians and citizens alike. When George Washington sought election to the Virginia House of Burgesses in 1757, he plied voters with 28 gallons of rum, 50 gallons of rum punch, 34 gallons of wine, 46 gallons of beer, and 2 gallons of cider. His opponents were quick to accuse him of buying votes. According to historian George Thayer, Washington's hospitality was considered a large campaign expenditure, since there were only 391 voters in his district.

When they sat down to write the Constitution of the United States, the Founding Fathers were certainly aware of the power of money in politics, but they did not anticipate how large a problem the financing of political campaigns would someday become. Neither did they foresee the rise of the highly competitive two-party political system, the growth in the number of elected officials, the expansion of the electorate to include women and blacks, the emergence of sophisticated and expensive communications media, or the development of nomination campaigns—all factors that influence campaign costs. The Constitution, therefore, does not directly address campaign financing, even though all political candidates since Washington's time have had to worry about campaign costs.

During the first half of the nineteenth century, most politicians conducted their campaigns through newspapers, pamphlets, and books. Voters were so deluged with printed matter that a writer in the *Charleston Gazette* protested, "We are so beset and run down by Federal republicans and their pamphlets that I begin to think . . . that there is rottenness in the system they attempt to support, or why all this violent electioneering?"[1] A "partisan press" quickly developed. To advance their ambitions, some politicians owned or controlled newspapers. These papers put forth only the views that supported their politicians, while at the same time mercilessly attacking their opponents.

By 1840, politicians had begun to use buttons, banners, pictures, and other novelties to reinforce their messages to the public. Political rallies and torchlight parades had also become increasingly popular. William Henry Harrison's presidential campaign that year had, as one observer noted, "conventions and mass meetings, parades and processions with banners and floats, long speeches on the log-cabin theme, log-cabin songbooks and log-cabin newspapers, Harrison pictures, and Tippecanoe handkerchiefs and badges."[2]

HARRISONIAN

BALL ROLLING.

KEEP THE

WILLIAM HENRY HARRISON — THE FARMER OF NORTH BEND.

RALLY!

A General Meeting

Will be held at the Old **COURT ROOM**, [Riey's building]

On Saturday Evening,

The 18th instant, at early candle light. A punctual atten-
dance is requested.

MESSRS. DAVIS, BOTKIN, KEATING

And others, will address the Meeting.

R. P. TODD, *Chairman*

July 17, 1840. *Vigilance Committee.*

*An 1840 campaign poster advertises
a rally in support of presidential
candidate William Henry Harrison.*

Although these innovative campaign techniques added to the costs of campaigning, it was not necessary to spend a great deal of money to wage a successful campaign. When Abraham Lincoln decided to run for Congress in 1846, his supporters raised $200 for his campaign fund. After winning the election, Lincoln returned $199.25 to his contributors, because he said he did not need the money. He used his own horse to ride to speeches, stayed in the homes of friends, and spent only 75 cents for a barrel of cider. In 1860, when Lincoln was elected president, his campaign cost about $100,000. A century later, when John F. Kennedy was elected, that amount would barely purchase one half hour of television time.[3] In all, Kennedy would spend one hundred times what Lincoln spent.

Early Concerns. Although few people worried about the costs of political campaigns, there was concern over the manner in which campaign chests were filled. On March 2, 1867, the first federal law on campaign financing was enacted as part of a bill on naval appropriations. The provision read: "No officer or employee of the government shall require or request any workingman in any navy yard to contribute or pay any money for political purposes, nor shall any workingman be removed or discharged for political opinion; and any officer or employee of the government who shall offend against the provisions of this section shall be dismissed from the service of the United States."

This law, however, had little effect on the "spoils system" that had gradually pervaded the government. In 1869 it was rumored that 75 percent of the money raised by the Republican Congressional Committee had come from people working in the federal government. In order to get—and keep—their civil service jobs, these people had been "encouraged" to contribute to the Republican coffers.

Public indignation about this practice led to the adoption of the Civil Service Reform Act of 1883, which, among other things, prohibited any federal employee from soliciting campaign funds from another federal employee.

But money could be found elsewhere. In the 1896 presidential contest between Republican William McKinley and Democrat William Jennings Bryan, McKinley's campaign was managed by a brilliant financier named Marcus A. Hanna. Using a strategy that pioneered the fund-raising techniques of later generations, Hanna turned his attention to banks, insurance companies, and large corporations. He assessed banks one quarter of one percent of their capital, and set quotas for contributions from businesses based on their ability to pay. From them he collected about $3.5 million—of which $250,000 came from John D. Rockefeller's Standard Oil Company alone.

By the beginning of the twentieth century, the increasing involvement of large corporations and financial institutions in campaign finance had begun to alarm many people. Among them were a group of dedicated reformers, known as "muckrakers," who agitated for campaign finance legislation and worked hard to expose the influence of unlimited spending by big business on the political campaigns of favored candidates and, ultimately, on the conduct of government. The reform movement also saw the formation of the National Publicity Law Association (NPLA), which numbered among its members such prominent figures as labor leader Samuel Gompers, presidential candidate William Jennings Bryan, and Charles Evans Hughes, who later became chief justice of the Supreme Court. The NPLA was a powerful voice in the call for reform legislation.

When President McKinley died in 1901, Vice President Theodore Roosevelt succeeded to the presidency. In his 1904 campaign for re-election, Roosevelt solicited

President William McKinley speaks from a bunting-draped stand at the 1901 Pan-American Exhibition. He was shot by an assassin the next day.

funds from two of the country's wealthiest men: E. H. Harriman and Henry Frick. Frick complained later that although Roosevelt had begged them for funds, once elected he would not stay "bought."

The Beginnings of Reform. Although Roosevelt received immense contributions from Harriman, Frick, and other wealthy individuals and corporations, he wasted little time in launching an attack on the men and the trusts who had supported him. He told Congress in 1907 that all contributions by corporations to any political committee or for any political purpose should be forbidden by law. He also proposed government funding of political campaigns. At the president's urging, Congress passed the Tillman Act in January 1907. The new legislation made it unlawful for a corporation or a national bank to make "a money contribution in connection with any election" of candidates for federal office.

Three years later, in 1910, Congress enacted legislation that established disclosure requirements for candidates for the House of Representatives. The new law required that political committees disclose the names of contributors and account for expenditures in a report to be filed with the clerk of the House within thirty days of the election. A law passed the following year, in 1911, extended the disclosure requirements to candidates for the Senate. The new legislation also set limits on the amount that House and Senate candidates could spend toward nomination and election: Candidates for the House could spend no more than $5,000, and candidates for the Senate could spend no more than $10,000. The law was later contested successfully in court. More than a decade was to elapse before Congress made any further attempt to regulate spending in federal campaigns.

A cartoon depicts Theodore Roosevelt as a lion tamer, forcing submission from the business trusts that dominated politics in his time.

The Federal Corrupt Practices Act. Finally, in 1925, the Federal Corrupt Practices Act (FCPA) was signed into law. The FCPA established new regulations for the disclosure of contributions and expenditures by candidates for the House and Senate (but not for the president or vice president), and by political committees that sought to influence federal elections in two or more states. It prohibited offering or giving money in exchange for votes.

The law also established new spending limits for federal candidates, but it was easy for candidates to get around the law. Because there was no restriction on the number of political committees that could contribute to a single campaign, all a candidate had to do was to establish multiple committees, each of which could then spend to the limit. And, because of the law's loosely defined disclosure requirements, congressional candidates often reported that they had neither received nor spent money on their campaigns, claiming that the committees working to elect them to office had operated without their knowledge or consent. The FCPA was, in fact, so riddled with loopholes that it was largely circumvented and ignored. Although it was widely recognized that many congressional candidates violated both the spending and disclosure provisions of the law, no one was ever prosecuted.

Despite its defects, the Federal Corrupt Practices Act served as the basic federal campaign finance law until 1972. It was amended several times. In a 1934 decision the Supreme Court ruled that the law was applicable to presidential elections, stating that, "public disclosure of political contributions, together with the names of contributors and other details, would tend to prevent the corrupt use of money to affect elections."

More Legislation and More Problems. While the country was still digging itself out of the Great Depression, Congress passed the Hatch Act of 1939 (also known as the Clean Politics Act), which prohibited the collection of campaign contributions from anyone receiving relief funds from the federal government and barred federal employees from actively participating in politics. A 1940 amendment to the Hatch Act added more teeth to the campaign finance law. It extended the regulations on campaign contributions to cover primary elections; it prohibited individuals from donating more than $5,000 to any federal candidate or political committee in any election; and it further prohibited businesses and individuals doing contract work for the government from contributing to any political candidate or committee. The law also imposed a tax on contributions of more than $3,000 to a single committee in any year, although it did not prevent individuals from giving that amount to numerous committees—all of which could be working for the same candidate. Thus, it was perfectly legal for an individual to give $100,000 or more to a single candidate—provided that the contribution was split up among a number of political committees, each of which was working for that candidate. However, individuals and businesses doing work for the federal government were prohibited from contributing to any candidate or political committee.

In 1943, while the nation was at war, Congress passed the Smith-Connally War Disputes Act, which extended to labor unions the ban on political contributions by corporations and national banks that had been on the books since 1907. The Taft-Hartley Act, which was signed into law in 1947, extended the ban on contributions by labor unions, corporations, and banks to cover primaries as well as general elections.

In the years following World War II, Congress made a few halfhearted gestures toward campaign finance reform, but no new legislation was enacted. The fact of the matter was that campaign contributions had become the well-traveled road for those seeking to buy political favors. Campaign giving—even illegal campaign giving—was so much easier than old-fashioned bribery. No one worried about the Federal Corrupt Practices Act, which, along with all its amendments, was unenforced and unenforceable. The FCPA had proved to be a failure. Incredibly, even open violations of the law were not prosecuted.

Nevertheless, everyone seemed satisfied until, by the 1960s, it became clear that the system of campaign financing was headed for disaster. The costs of campaigns had begun to soar, and candidates searched desperately for more and more funds. Vast amounts of money began pouring into political coffers, and with the flow of dollars came the opportunity for large-scale political corruption.

Postwar Reforms. John F. Kennedy, who was elected president in 1960, took the first serious steps toward reform. As a member of a wealthy and politically powerful family, Kennedy was aware of the advantages that personal wealth could give to a candidate. Because he himself had been accused of buying his way into office, Kennedy was especially sensitive to possible abuses in campaign finance and was determined to bring about reforms in the system. At his urging a committee—the Commission on Campaign Costs—was formed to study the problem. In its 1962 report, the commission presented a comprehensive program for reforming the financing of the entire political system from the federal level on down. For example, it recommended that ways should be found to encourage more people to contribute, thus ensuring candidates enough money without the possibility of undue influence by a few large contributors; and it urged full disclosure of primary as well as general election contributions. But Congress was slow to respond. Why, after all, should they change the rules of the game when they had been elected and re-elected under the old financial rules? Indeed, more than twelve years were to pass before some of the commission's proposals—such as public matching funds for presidential candidates—were adopted.

But Congress was finally impelled to act because of the sudden, steep rise in costs of political campaigns. Throughout the 1960s, the continuing escalation in campaign costs and the demand for ever larger war chests exaggerated all the problems inherent in the system and brought them to the attention of "good government" and "public interest" groups, and to elected officials as well.

In 1967, President Lyndon Johnson brought the subject of campaign finance reform to the attention of the nation, calling for tax incentives for small contributions, the removal of unrealistic spending ceilings, and full disclosure of contributions and expenditures. Johnson criticized the Federal Corrupt Practices Act and the Hatch Act, asserting that they were inadequate when enacted and had become obsolete, and that their loopholes invited evasion of the law. The question was no longer whether campaign finance laws should be changed, but how they should be changed.

By 1970 major reforms were under way at all levels of government. Surprisingly, it was the states—led by Colorado and Washington—that enacted the most sweeping reform legislation. Nearly all of them took significant action to reduce the influence of money and secrecy on their political processes.

At the federal level, the first attempt at reform occurred in 1970 with the passage by Congress of a new but somewhat narrow campaign finance law. Hardly anyone on Capitol Hill was upset, however, when President Richard M. Nixon vetoed the bill. He had, after all, promised to support an improved version during the next session of Congress.

What did alarm Congress was a Supreme Court ruling concerning Common Cause, the citizens' lobby that long has urged reform of campaign finance laws. In 1971, Common Cause sued both the Republican and Democratic parties for violating the Federal Corrupt Practices Act of 1925 and the Supreme Court ruled that the citizens' group had standing—that is, it had the right to bring such a suit. Decades had passed in which a succession of attorneys general had failed to enforce the law. Now the Supreme Court had sanctioned the right of citizens to seek enforcement of campaign finance laws—thus opening an alternative means of routing out dishonesty and corruption.

The members of Congress acted quickly to repeal the provision in the FCPA that set a $5,000 ceiling on political contributions from any individual. They had ignored or circumvented the ceiling for more than thirty years, secure in the knowledge that the Department of Justice would not enforce the law. Now that enforcement could come from another direction—namely, citizen litigation—they realized that the "good old days" were over.

Landmark Legislation. In 1971, Congress passed two pieces of legislation designed to overhaul the campaign finance system—the Federal Election Campaign Act (FECA), which, as previously mentioned, set limits on the amount that federal candidates could spend on media advertising and required full disclosure of campaign contributions and expenditures; and the Revenue Act of 1971, which allowed taxpayers to contribute to a general campaign fund for eligible presidential and vice presidential candidates by checking off a box on their income tax forms.

The public reporting requirements of the 1971 laws did not prevent the large illegal donations of the Watergate scandal. Evidence of the huge number of illegal campaign contributions given by individuals and corporations dem-

Common Cause chairman John Gardner at a 1972 news conference. The citizens' group sued both major political parties for violating campaign financing laws.

onstrated to both voters and lawmakers the need for more far-reaching campaign finance reforms. In reaction to these presidential campaign abuses, Congress passed the historic reform law of 1974. Technically, the 1974 law was a set of amendments to the FECA of 1971, but it was, in fact, the most comprehensive and thorough campaign finance legislation ever enacted. The new law, for the first time, set spending limits for candidates in presidential primary and general elections. It also set spending limits for House and Senate candidates. And it set limits on the amounts that individuals, organizations, political committees, state and national political party organizations, as well as candidates themselves could contribute in primaries and general elections. Stiff disclosure and enforcement rules were also included, and the 1971 media spending limitations were repealed.

Most important, the 1974 law provided for the use of public funds to finance presidential elections—a concept first raised many years before by Theodore Roosevelt—and established federal matching grants to cover up to one-half of the costs of presidential primary campaigns. It also created the bipartisan Federal Election Commission (FEC) to administer election laws.

Buckley *v.* Valeo. Further amendments were added to the law in 1976 following a Supreme Court decision in the case known as *Buckley* v. *Valeo*. Shortly after the 1974 law took effect, it was challenged by a group of plaintiffs, including Senators James L. Buckley and Eugene J. McCarthy, who argued that the public financing provisions of the law discriminated against minor parties and lesser-known candidates, and that the limits on campaign contributions and expenditures prevented candidates and contributors from expressing themselves freely in the political arena. They were concerned that the reforms would have a chilling effect on free speech and on the free participation of ordinary citizens. Thus, the problem for the court was to balance First Amendment rights of free speech and free association against the power of the legislature to enact laws meant to protect the integrity of the election system.

The decision of the Court upheld the provisions of the law that set limits on how much individuals and political committees could contribute to a candidate, provided for public financing of presidential campaigns, and required disclosure of contributions of more than $10 and campaign expenditures of more than $100.

In overturning other portions of the law, however, the Court ruled that campaign spending limits violated the First Amendment guarantee of free speech, except in the case of presidential candidates who accepted federal matching funds. In its written decision, the Court stated that spending caps restrict a candidate's ability to communicate freely with voters, "because virtually every means of communicating ideas in today's mass society requires the expenditure of money." In comparing the provisions covering contribution and spending limits, the Court stated that the law's "expenditure ceilings impose significantly more severe restrictions on protected freedom of political expression and association than do its limitations on financial contributions."[4]

The law had also limited the amount of money that candidates could spend on their own campaigns. In striking down these provisions, the Court commented, "The candidate, no less than any other person, has a First Amendment right to engage in the discussion of public issues and vigorously and tirelessly to advocate his own election and the election of other candidates." This made it possible for wealthy candidates to finance their own campaigns, thus avoiding the limits on contributions from others. "The use of personal funds," the Court stated, "reduces the candidate's dependence on outside contributions and thereby counteracts the coercive pressures and attendant risks of abuse to which the Act's contribution limits are directed."[5]

But Associate Justices Byron White and Thurgood Marshall disagreed with the majority opinion. Marshall said that limits on personal spending do not deny a candidate's ability to speak and spend freely. He also wrote that a candidate with a large personal fortune would be off to a "head start" compared with other candidates. "The perception that personal wealth wins elections may not only discourage potential candidates without significant personal wealth from entering the political arena, but also undermine public confidence in the integrity of the electoral process," Marshall wrote.[6]

In all cases the Court ruled that limits on campaign spending violated the First Amendment, but by removing these ceilings, the Court effectively reduced the impact of those portions of the law that placed limits on contributions. Justice Marshall feared that upholding the limits on contributions while striking those on spending "put a premium on a candidate's personal wealth."

No one was completely satisfied with the decision, but it allowed both sides at the time to at least claim a partial victory. John Gardner of Common Cause, for example, felt the ruling rewarded all those who had worked to clean up the political process.

Congress, however, had its work cut out for it. Chief Justice Warren E. Burger, in a separate dissent, complained that the decision was unworkable. Most observers today agree. "The result was the worst of all worlds," commented former senator James L. Buckley, one of the plaintiffs who challenged the law. "We ended up with legislation on the books that created the problems we face today and limited means to address them."[7]

The Court's ruling had left standing a set of ground rules that were in need of immediate revision. In 1976, Congress passed amendments to the law, which reopened the door to large contributions through political action committees and generally broadened the limits on contributions. In 1979, Congress added more amendments that essentially "fine-tuned" the operation of the Federal Election Commission, as well as the provisions dealing with disclosure.

Although the campaign finance reform legislation of the 1970s solved some old problems, it also gave birth to new ones. In attempting to prevent wealthy individuals from "buying" candidates and from exerting undue influence on political outcomes, it created a new monster in the form of political action committees—the new legally sanctioned mechanisms designed to handle special-interest contributions.

The growth of political action committees parallels the dramatic rise in campaign costs beginning in the 1970s. For example, according to the FEC, winning congressional candidates in 1992 spent more than six times what victors spent in 1978.[8] At the same time, the new law limited the role of major contributors and forced candidates to appeal to large numbers of voters in order to raise sufficient funds. In their desperate scramble for money, candidates have been forced to rely increasingly on contributions from special-interest groups. When he was asked why he robbed banks, the famous bank robber Willie Sutton answered, "Because that's where the money is!" If asked why they seek support from political action committees, most politicians would give the same answer.

In the next chapter, we will take a closer look at the phenomenon of political action committees and the role they play in the electoral process.

4 The Rise of Political Action Committees

Political action committees, or PACs, are special-interest groups that, although not authorized by candidates or political parties, give money to candidates for public office. They consist of groups of people, who, instead of donating directly to candidates of their choice, pool their money in order to contribute it to candidates or political party committees who share their particular political, social, religious, philosophical, or economic views. By combining their many small contributions into larger, more meaningful amounts, PAC members are able to pursue their objectives more effectively than if each member acted independently.

PACs fall into four broad categories: (1) associations composed of people in the same business or profession, such as doctors, lawyers, real estate brokers, insurance agents, dairy farmers, bankers, or auto dealers; (2) trade unions such as the Teamsters' Union, the United Auto Workers, the AFL-CIO, or the United Mine Workers; (3) groups composed of political conservatives or liberals, or people who share the same ideological views about women's rights, abortion, the environment, civil rights, gun control, support for Israel, or other issues; and (4) corporations such as U.S. Steel, Lockheed, Mobil, J. C. Penney, Philip Morris, and so on. Today, almost every special-interest group has a PAC—from defense contractors to letter carriers to environmentalists. Even beer wholesalers have their own political action committee, which at one time they referred to as SIXPAC.

Unlike party committees, which are directly affiliated with political parties, PACs are "nonparty" organizations. A PAC cannot be formed by, or directly connected to, a political party, even if all its contributions are given to candidates of a single party. The law requires PACs to disclose how much and to whom they contribute. Disclosure reports are filed with the FEC, the regulatory agency that enforces the law. The reports become public record.

The law also regulates the manner in which PACs can solicit contributions from their members, employees, and shareholders. Most PACs solicit donations from their members once a year. To collect contributions from members, corporate PACs sometimes use a "checkoff" system in which contributions are deducted automatically from members' paychecks. The typical PAC member's contribution is under $200.

Although the law prohibits an individual from giving more than a total of $25,000 to all federal candidates in any election, there is no legal limit on the total amount a PAC can give. A PAC is allowed to donate up to $10,000 to an individual candidate in a federal election ($5,000 in the primary and another $5,000 in the general election), provided the PAC has been registered with the Federal Election Commission for at least six months, has more than fifty members, and has supported five or more candidates.

Staggering amounts of PAC money have poured into congressional campaigns. In this cartoon, the Capitol is a coin bank for wealthy special interests.

There is, however, no limit to the number of candidates to whom a PAC can contribute. Thus, a PAC may give $10,000 to each of a number of congressional candidates. As a result, PACs are responsible for pouring staggering amounts of money into political campaigns. In the 1992 election, for example, the FEC reported that candidates for Senate and House seats received a total of $180.4

million from PACs. Contributions to Senate campaigns reached $51.8 million, while House donations were $128.6 million.[1]

The Growth of PACs. Why and how did PACs originate? Special-interest organizations, of which PACs are one form, have always played an important role in American politics. In fact, the habit of forming clubs and organizations with people of like interests in order to achieve certain goals seems to be a particular American trait. The French writer Alexis de Tocqueville noticed this during a visit to the United States in the 1830s. "Americans of all ages, all conditions, and all dispositions, constantly form associations," he wrote. "Wherever at the head of some new undertaking you see the government in France, or a man of rank in England, in the United States you will be sure to find an association."[2]

Since their activities are often affected by laws and regulations, and they seek to achieve some of their goals through governmental action, it is not surprising that special-interest groups try to influence public officials to act in their favor. One of their most potent weapons is campaign contributions. Indeed, throughout American history, special-interest groups have poured cash—and lots of it— into the campaign chests of political candidates.

By targeting campaign donations, special-interest groups hope to gain access to politicians who have the power to influence legislation or regulation governing their area of concern. Once they have a politician's ear, they hope to convince that person to act in ways that will promote the group's goals and interests. Although there is nothing inherently wrong with this, problems can and do arise when the narrow interests of a group are not consistent with the broader interests of society as a whole.

In a democracy, elected officials are responsible for

weighing the competing interests and desires of all segments of society, and reaching decisions that are in the best
interests of the majority of the people. This decision-
making process is not always easy. For example, placing
high tariffs on imported sugar may please domestic sugar
growers, but American consumers will have to pay more
for the product at the grocery store. In order to reach a
balanced decision, politicians have to weigh the interests of
domestic sugar growers against those of consumers, while
determining what is best for the nation as a whole.

The Origin of PACs. Political action committees had their
origins not in the business community but in the labor
movement. The first PAC was formed in 1943 when the
Congress of Industrial Organizations (CIO) established its
CIO-PAC to give "muscle" to the voluntary political contributions of union members. The idea was to amass the
small gifts of individuals and donate the total to politicians
helpful to working people. In 1947 the American Federa-
tion of Labor (AFL), the country's other major labor organization, followed suit with the establishment of its own
PAC. When, in 1955, these two giant union federations
united to form the AFL–CIO, their PACs merged as well.
This powerful PAC not only was able to pour millions of
dollars into political campaigns, but it also provided man-
power to favored candidates, conducted voter registration
campaigns, and organized effective get-out-the-vote drives
on election day.

Business interests felt threatened by the powerful labor PACs until they realized that they, too, could use PACs
to further their own goals. Corporations especially em-
braced the PAC concept as a replacement for the sometimes dubious fund-raising methods they had used in the
past. In 1962 the American Medical Political Action Committee (AMPAC) was formed, followed in 1963 by the

Business-Industry Political Action Committee (BIPAC). It wasn't long before business PACs were able to match the strength of their opponents in the labor movement. By 1964 the number of business PACs had grown to eleven.

As the cost of campaigns continued to shoot skyward throughout the 1970s and 1980s, politicians became increasingly obsessed with money. Since there were no legal limits on the amount of money that could be spent in a campaign, candidates worried more and more about being outspent by their opponents. In their frantic search for money, they began to rely more and more heavily on PACs.

Although PACs had been active for about thirty years, it was during the 1970s—the decade of campaign finance reform—that they began to multiply. In 1974 there were 608 PACs registered with the FEC. By 1988 the number of registered PACs had grown to 4,268. The amount of their giving also increased. PAC contributions to congressional candidates were about $8.5 million in 1972, $55.2 million in 1980 and $151.3 million in 1988.[3] Although their donations went up in 1992, PACs actually covered a smaller share of total candidate spending. In the House, political action committees paid for 37.1 percent of all election expenses, compared with 41.4 percent in 1990. The share of election costs paid by political-action committees in the Senate stayed about the same.[4]

The PAC Debate. It is not surprising that in their search for campaign funds politicians have found PACs irresistible. The ability of PACs to collect money and offer large chunks of it to many candidates makes them particularly attractive to politicians in search of shortcuts.

The concern about the infusion of PAC money into the American political scene has given rise to a spirited debate. Defenders of the system insist that there is no cause for alarm. They point to the fact that PAC campaign contributions make it possible for candidates of modest means to compete with wealthier opponents, especially incumbents. They say that, since PACs are prohibited by law from giving more than $10,000 to any single candidate, it is silly to suppose that PACs can unduly influence the way a politician thinks and votes. Those who defend the system also argue that PACs allow ordinary people to make their voices heard. "The fact is that the Political Action Committee movement is a *reform movement itself,*" said Senator Richard Lugar. "It is a straightforward way in which many individuals make small contributions and work in concert to achieve ends in which they believe. It is the antithesis of back-room politics."[5]

But critics of the system disagree. PACs, they say, have one objective: to gain influence with, or favored access to, elected officials. This influence-buying motive has led to some questionable—even shocking—practices. Although defenders of the system say that PAC money helps newcomers of modest means to challenge incumbents, critics point out that PAC money is seldom given to challengers. Indeed, the record shows that in the 1986 elections for the House of Representatives, more than 88 percent of PAC contributions went to incumbents, while fewer than 12 percent went to challengers. This practice is nothing new: since 1974, PAC donations have been contributed overwhelmingly to incumbent politicians. According to Common Cause, in the 1992 elections PACs gave incumbents more than $119 million, compared with the $17 million they gave challengers.[6] No matter what their party, incumbents in 1992 raised ten times more PAC money than their opponents.[7]

According to proponents of the system, PACs foster voluntary participation of ordinary citizens in the political process. They argue that, by uniting the voices and monetary contributions of like-minded individuals, PAC members stand a much better chance of having their concerns heard. PAC funds represent the collective voice of many people who share the same interests, and thus have a much greater impact on politicians than do the voices of individual small contributors.

But are all PAC funds made up of voluntary contributions? Not so, say some critics. They point out that, although most PACs use aboveboard methods, the manner in which some PACs collect money from their members can verge on coercion. For instance, some corporate PACs set "suggested" contribution quotas based on employees' salaries. One company gave bonuses of $2,000 to $2,500 to key management personnel, along with a firm suggestion and printed request that a PAC contribution would be appreciated.[8] A few labor PACs have used similar tactics to encourage contributions from union members.

Another problem is the manner in which PACs decide how much and to which candidates they are going to contribute. PAC members have little or no say concerning who should benefit from PAC donations. In most PACs these decisions are made by a small committee or board of directors. People who make contributions through PACs essentially surrender control of their money. Thus, instead of fostering citizen participation in the political process, PACs relieve their members from personal involvement.

In most instances the manner in which PACs give money leaves little doubt that their motive is to gain access and influence. By and large, contributions go to politicians useful to the special needs or goals of the PAC. In 1986, for example, PACs allied with banks and financial institutions "invested" more than $3.4 million in members of House and Senate banking committees. PACs sometimes give to both candidates in an election. For example, certain PACs gave money to both Ronald Reagan and Walter Mondale in the 1984 presidential election. PACs also give money to candidates whose principles and philosophies they don't share. And sometimes, if the candidate they back ends up a loser, PACs may turn around and donate money to the winner—after the election is over.

PACs often support candidates who have no need for money and who have no opponent. In his book *The Best Congress Money Can Buy*, author Philip M. Stern describes how New York representative Charles Rangel was continually showered with PAC contributions, despite the fact that he had been re-elected time and time again by an overwhelming majority and was virtually unopposed in his Harlem district. According to an FEC press release in March 1993, Rangel in 1992 received 95 percent of the vote and more than $300,000 in PAC funds.[9] When the election was over, Rangel still had about $174,000 left in his campaign chest. When he leaves the Congress, Rangel can legally take any surplus campaign funds with him.

To the average citizen, the idea of contributing to a politician who faces no opposition and who doesn't need campaign funds makes no sense at all. Why, then, do PACs continue to give money to these surefire winners? The answer is simple. PACs support those politicians who have the power to affect legislation governing the group's interests. Congressman Rangel, for example, was a powerful member of the House Ways and Means Committee, which writes tax laws. When, in 1985, the committee was working on a reform bill that threatened to wipe out tax loopholes that were worth billions of dollars to businesses and industries, business and industry PACs decided to give money to Rangel's campaign. If they could persuade Rangel to listen to them and if he could be convinced to act in their favor, the $300,000 they contributed to his campaign would be a small price to pay compared with the billions in tax dollars these industries would save.

Representative Rangel, however, was far from the only recipient of PAC money, nor was he the top PAC recipient in the 1992 congressional campaign. Senator Wayne Fowler of Georgia received $1,592,996, while twenty other Senate candidates also received over a million dollars each from PACs. House Majority Leader Richard Gephardt received $1,240,597.[10] Gephardt's colleague House Speaker Thomas Foley received 74 percent of his total campaign funds from PACs.[11]

In their attempt to gain influence or favored access, most PACs target funds to members of Congress who serve on committees closely tied to their interests. During the 1988 campaign, for example, congressional candidates received $27 million from PACs representing finance, real estate, and insurance companies—$3.8 million of which went to members of the Senate Finance Committee alone. In the same year, members of the House Agriculture Committee received $2 million from agriculture PACs. According to Common Cause, from January 1981 through June 1991, medical industry PACs gave $60 million to congressional candidates.[12] During this time, although overall PAC contributions to congressional campaigns increased by 90 percent, medical industry contributions jumped 140 percent.[13]

With a few outstanding exceptions, nearly all members of the Senate and House have accepted PAC campaign contributions. In the 1980 elections, PACs contributed a total of $10.2 million to the winners in Senate races; by 1992, PAC contributions to winners climbed to $31.8 million. In 1980 winners of House seats received $27 million from PACs; in 1992, PAC contributions to winners had mushroomed to $97.2 million.[14] *The New York Times* has called Congress "PAC-addicted," citing the statistic that of the $190 million raised by House incumbents in the 1992 elections, nearly half came from PACs.[15]

That PACs contribute vast amounts of money to political campaigns is borne out by the figures above. Critics contend that our lawmakers are so indebted to special-interest PACs that they cannot adequately run the nation. They also charge that PACs engage in a variety of highly questionable activities in their efforts to dominate elections and influence elected officials. For example, PACs have been criticized for "bundling." In this practice, individuals and PACs that have already given the maximum to a candidate then give more money to an intermediary, who passes the contributions along to the same candidate.

Is it true that PACs are buying not only access but votes as well? Is it true that our elected officials are for sale? These disturbing questions will be explored in the next chapter.

5

Buying Access
or
Buying Votes?

Money, in the form of contributions, is the lifeblood of any political campaign. With enough money, candidates can get their messages across to large numbers of voters. Without money, candidates cannot compete effectively in a system of free elections. About 500,000 public offices—from local dogcatcher to president of the United States—are filled by election, and each of these campaigns requires money.[1]

Since few federal candidates are wealthy enough to finance their own campaigns, most candidates must solicit funds from outside sources. As we have seen, millions of dollars are poured directly into campaigns by wealthy individuals and PACs. Additional millions are poured into the coffers of both the Republican and Democratic parties in the form of "soft money" contributions. Soft money is supposed to be used for party-building activities but often ends up supporting the campaigns of individual candidates.

The torrents of money flowing into campaigns have triggered some disturbing questions. Do campaign contributions influence the way our elected officials deal with issues that concern the nation? What must politicians do to keep contributions coming in? Where is the line between "buying access" and "buying votes"? According to political writer Elizabeth Drew:

The current system is one of legalized corruption. In order to amass the ever-growing amounts of funds that the politicians need (or think they need) to win an election, they put themselves in hock to the interests (liberal as well as conservative) that can donate substantial funds. In return, they then are often inclined to do the things donors want and not to move on the things they don't want. Technically, it's not bribery, but it's awfully close.[2]

Critics of the campaign finance system contend that PACs and wealthy individuals don't give large campaign contributions out of the goodness of their hearts—they expect something in return. In March 1993, Senator David Boren, a leader in the fight to reform campaign financing, told a Senate committee: "Our constituents know what happens when there's someone who's able to control the flow of PAC money waiting to see us, and you have five minutes to see one person or another, and six or eight constituents are also competing for our time, and we're desperate to raise all that campaign money."[3]

Another critic, former representative William Broadhead of Michigan, said: "Why do you think the biggest, brightest business people in America are raising millions of dollars to give to members of Congress? They're trying to buy votes. There's no other purpose to it. Labor unions, trade associations are all doing the same thing."[4]

Former president Ronald Reagan dismissed criticism of PACs as a tactic of the political opposition. "I'm a little amused that suddenly our opponents have developed a real conscience about political action committees," he said. "I

Lobbyists line a Capitol hallway during congressional budget hearings. Reporters have nicknamed the hall "Gucci Gulch" for the crowds of well-dressed lobbyists that gather there.

don't remember them being that aroused when the only ones that you knew about were on their side. Now they're on our side and they want to do away with them. Well, they're not going to do away with [them]."[5]

The late Justin Dart, former chairman of Dart Industries, a PAC spokesman and longtime friend of Reagan, claimed that contributions simply buy access. "Talking to politicians is a fine thing," he said, "but with a little money they hear you better."[6]

Most Americans, however, believe that as long as their elected officials listen to PACs and big money donors, they can't or won't hear what ordinary voters have to say. According to one Gallup poll, 71 percent of those surveyed think that most members of Congress are more interested in serving special-interest groups than the public. Who is right?

To answer that question, let's look at the way business PACs operate. Each of these PACs represents a certain industry, such as real estate or banking or insurance or health care or the defense industry. In Congress, usually one or two committees and subcommittees oversee the activities of each industry. For example, the banking committees in the House and Senate supervise how banks do business; the energy committees supervise the oil, gas, and chemical industries; the defense committees approve funds for military equipment. In this way, each industry has its "own" lawmakers—a handful of senators and congressmen who determine the laws that regulate the industry, and who have a powerful influence on its future.

To ensure that "their" senators and congressmen will deal favorably with issues facing their particular industry, PACs use a two-pronged approach. First, they develop personal relationships with "their" candidates; second, they contribute funds to "their" candidates' campaigns.

For example, suppose that a defense contractor wants to obtain a highly profitable helicopter contract with the government. In a meeting with "his" congressional representatives, a member of the contractor's PAC emphasizes how important the helicopter is to national defense, and, incidentally, how important the contract would be to the economic health of his company. Although no one may actually say so, it is understood that the senator or House member who votes to give the contract to the company will almost certainly receive a large campaign contribution. When the senator or representative votes "yes," he or she can defend this action by saying that it serves the national interest. A "no" vote, however, may jeopardize future campaign contributions from the contractor's PAC.

Every year, hundreds of "deals" such as this take place. In 1985, for example, every member of the House Defense Appropriations subcommittee, the group that approves funds for arms projects, received contributions from the PAC belonging to General Dynamics, a large military contractor.

Some people see nothing wrong with politicians receiving such campaign contributions as long as the public interest is being served. In the example given above, it can be argued that helicopters and other military equipment are necessary, so what difference does it make if politicians accept campaign contributions from defense contractors who just happen to want to make money? After all, such contributions are legal.

The Savings and Loan Debacle. But many people maintain that the public interest is not always being served by such deals. The Savings and Loan (S&L) crisis is a case in point. Originally, savings and loan institutions (also called "thrifts") were places where people could invest money in savings accounts. This money in turn was lent to other people for home mortgages. Thrift operations were regulated by the government, and every depositor's account was insured for up to $100,000 by the government's Federal Savings and Loan Insurance Corporation (FSLIC).

In the 1980s certain regulations governing the operation of S&Ls were lifted, and their doors were opened to what many now believe was the largest financial scandal in history. Thrift industry lobbyists said that if these regulations were lifted, S&Ls could make loans to builders. This would boost the economy and create new jobs.

The fact that the S&Ls were also waving around a lot of money made these ideas even more attractive. *The New York Times* recognized that many powerful congressional leaders were taken in by the savings and loan executives from their states and were certainly influenced by their quest for campaign donations. As the *Washington Post* noted, "The S&Ls were a prolific source of campaign contributions." Thus, during the 1980s, while S&L institutions nationwide were engaging in activities that led to their collapse, S&L interests gave $11.6 million in campaign contributions to candidates and political party committees.

After deregulation, many S&Ls invested in highly speculative ventures instead of simply lending money to home buyers as they traditionally had done. What followed was, in the words of Attorney General Richard Thornburgh, an "epidemic of fraud." The failure of unsafe investments, along with mismanagement and a host of illegal activities, caused hundreds of S&L institutions to close their doors. The federal government, which had insured the savings of S&L depositors, was stuck with the bill. Where would the government get the money? From taxpayers, of course.

In November 1990, the dimensions of the scandal began to be revealed when Charles H. Keating, Jr., officer of a California thrift organization, was arrested on criminal

Senator Alan Cranston confers with his lawyer Alan Dershowitz in November 1990, just after he was reprimanded for his involvement with Lincoln Savings & Loan.

fraud charges. His association with five respected members of Congress then came under investigation. It was alleged that, in return for $1.3 million in contributions to their political campaigns, these men—the "Keating Five"— used their political power to influence government regulators on behalf of Keating's Lincoln Savings & Loan Association. Keating subsequently was convicted, and one of the senators, Alan Cranston of California, was reprimanded by the Senate Ethics Committee for his role in the affair.

Senator Cranston, however, didn't take the reprimand lying down. He told committee members he had ample evidence to demonstrate to both the Senate and the nation that there were many examples of similar conduct. He maintained that his behavior did not violate the established norms of behavior and that members of both political parties were involved.

American voters have cause for frustration as they face the tax bill generated by the S&L bailout. Some experts say that the cost to taxpayers will run as high as $1.4 trillion—more than $5,600 for every man, woman, and child in the country. It's hard to comprehend a sum of money this large. But using an S&L term, housing, as a comparison may help. In 1992 the median price of a house in the United States was $100,900.[7] By rounding off the figures, we see that $1.4 trillion is enough to build and give away nearly 14 million homes. That means that we could give a free home to every single family in New York City, Los Angeles, Chicago, Houston, Philadelphia, San Diego, Dallas, Phoenix, Detroit, and at least a dozen other cities.

"The theft from the taxpayer by the community that fattened on the growth of the savings and loan (S&L) industry in the 1980s is the worst public scandal in American history," wrote Martin Mayer in his book *The Greatest-Ever Bank Robbery: The Collapse of the Savings and Loan Industry*. "Political analysts have already seen the S&L crisis as an illustration of the corruption that must ultimately infect any government where the costs of running for office are greater than those that can or will be borne by the relatively small community of the public-spirited."[8]

Americans were angry. Those who betrayed the public trust, whether elected official or banker, would probably never pay for all their crimes. Nor was it likely that the stolen money would be confiscated and returned to the U.S. Treasury and taxpayers. The best voters could hope for was that steps would be taken to prevent such a scandal from happening again. Thus, if there is one positive result of the S&L disaster, it is that it has focused public concern and given new impetus to the ongoing debate over campaign finance reform.

Is Democracy in Danger?

Democracy is a form of government in which supreme political power is vested in the people. In the United States that power is exercised through a system of representative government in which politicians, who are supposed to represent the will of the people, gain office through regular free elections. All citizens of voting age have the right to vote for the candidates of their choice. And the vote of one citizen is supposed to count as much as that of any other citizen—regardless of their economic, social, or other individual differences. Guaranteed by the Constitution, the cherished right of "one person, one vote" is the cornerstone of the American political system.

The oldest, most successful continuing democracy in the world, the United States serves as a model of freedom to millions of people who regard the right to vote as a precious weapon in the struggle to bring democracy to their own societies. In the United States, however, many citizens seem to take the right to vote for granted.

Among the world's democracies, the United States ranks near the bottom in its rate of voter participation in the electoral process. Since 1972 only 50 to 55 percent of eligible voters have bothered to vote in the presidential elections, which are held every four years. In "off" year elections—that is, elections in which candidates are running for offices other than the presidency—voter turnout hovers between 36 and 40 percent.

Why do so many American voters fail to exercise their rights? According to some analysts, Americans don't vote because they are satisfied with things as they are and see no need for change, or because they are too busy or too wrapped up in their own affairs to care about what happens in government.

Although some Americans may be so happy with the status quo that they fail to vote, many political observers believe that voter apathy has its roots in other causes. They point to mounting evidence that voters are repelled by the choices and disgusted with the conduct of government. Many voters, they say, are angry, frustrated, and alienated. When these voters look at their government, they don't like what they see but feel powerless to change anything. They feel, quite simply, that their votes don't count.

Many citizens are convinced that no matter who is elected, that person will be indebted to the special-interest groups that financed the campaign. Voters feel that they cannot compete effectively with these special-interest groups for the attention of their elected leaders.

While political action committees and other special-interest groups are able to use campaign contributions to command the attention of politicians, ordinary citizens have few means of influencing the decision-making that will affect their lives. Drowned out by the roar of special-interest money pouring into campaign chests, they cannot make their voices heard on such important matters as how their taxes are spent, how the economy is regulated, and how problems such as unemployment and health care are

Voters line up at a New York City polling place. Voter turnout has dropped as people have become disillusioned with politics.

dealt with. While special-interest groups are granted tax breaks, subsidies, and special concessions of one kind or another, the needs of ordinary voters are ignored. Through higher taxes and prices, all Americans do, however, pay the bill for many of the deals made between the special-interest groups and elected officials.

It is not surprising, therefore, that when given the opportunity to tell how they really feel about politics and politicians, many Americans register disgust and anger. Nor is it surprising that the sense of alienation among voters is growing. Alienation should concern us all. Democracy cannot flourish under a system that offers special-interest groups unlimited opportunities to gain access to the corridors of power, while ordinary citizens are locked out at the gates.

Fred Wertheimer, president of Common Cause, called the situation, "Alarming. Outrageous. Downright dangerous. That's the only way to begin to describe the threat posted by the torrents of special interest campaign cash being offered up to our Representatives and Senators.... This democracy-threatening trend must stop."[1]

Does the current system of campaign financing threaten to undermine our political processes as Wertheimer warns? Wertheimer quotes Professor Frank J. Sorauf of the University of Minnesota, who said that "even writing a check or giving cash to a PAC is a somewhat limited form of participation that requires little time or immediate involvement ..." and that "it is one of the least active forms of political activity, well suited to the very busy or to those who find politics strange, boring, or distasteful."[2] John Kerry reported in *The Congressional Digest* in February 1987 that "our democratic system is slowly being corroded and eroded by the influence of PAC money. As the amount of PAC money increases, our credibility and our appearance of integrity decreases."[3]

Money is a symbol of the deeper competition for political power. Because money is so unevenly distributed, it is a poor tool of democracy. Doctors, lawyers, realtors, corporations, and other affluent groups exercise immense political clout by means of their PAC contributions. But many people believe the growth of PACs has resulted in unbalanced representation in Congress. As former senator Gary Hart of Colorado told the Senate, "It seems the only group without a well-heeled PAC is the average citizen—the voter who has no special interest beyond low taxes, an efficient government, an honorable Congress, and a humane society. Those are the demands we should be heeding—but those are the demands the PACs have drowned out."[4]

Others are not so sure. Senate minority leader Robert Dole remarked, "There aren't any poor PACs or Food Stamp PACs or Nutrition PACs or Medicare PACs."[5] Nevertheless, without support from PACs, there are food stamps, nutrition and poverty programs, and Medicare. Their existence is cited as evidence that votes are more important to elected officials than money.

Moreover, not everyone sees PACs as a threat to democracy. Larry J. Sabato, a professor of government and specialist in the development of PACs, commented that "PACs will never be popular with idealistic reformers because they represent the rough, cutting edge of a democracy teeming with different peoples and conflicting interests."[6] Sabato contended that PACs have taken the place in the public's mind of the "fat cat" political bosses of the turn of the century and symbolize the role of money in politics. Americans seem to have a native distrust of mixing money and politics. Therefore, PACs, as the symbol of "dirty political money," have inherited all the suspicions that are typically held by those who want to keep dollars and democracy separate.

Still, many people believe that the current system of campaign financing imperils democracy in numerous ways:

- Because campaigns are so expensive, money often determines who shall run for office. If a modern Abraham Lincoln were to run for office today, his chances would be slim unless his campaign were bankrolled by wealthy individuals and special-interest groups.
- The need to raise campaign money prevents lawmakers from doing their jobs effectively. Were it not for this need, the time and energy spent crisscrossing the country in pursuit of campaign funds could otherwise be spent doing the jobs they were elected to do.
- Big-money contributors often determine what messages will be most forcefully conveyed to voters. Money gives people the power to be heard.
- When politicians accept special-interest funds, they may obligate themselves to give favored treatment to special-interest lobbyists. There is an old saying: "He who pays the piper calls the tune." In the context of politics, this means that politicians often feel obligated to promote the interests of those who financed their campaigns.
- The PAC system is costly to ordinary citizens. For business and industry, campaign contributions are part of the cost of doing business and as such are built into the price of products that consumers buy. Moreover, special-interest influence often results in subsidies, tax breaks, and other benefits that are ultimately paid for by ordinary taxpayers.
- The system lacks the safeguards necessary to prevent unscrupulous individuals from using it

for their own gain. Current law sets no limits on the amount of money candidates can amass—and it allows candidates to keep whatever funds are left after the campaign bills are paid. The temptation to manipulate the system for personal profit has proved irresistible to some.

Is the United States the only country facing these problems? Have other democracies handled the problems of campaign financing differently? Some have stricter laws, while others have few regulations. A look at campaign financing in three other nations may shed some light on how Americans might solve the current problems.

United Kingdom. As in the United States, elections in the United Kingdom are dominated by the competition between two major parties, Conservative and Labour. Unlike our Republicans and Democrats, however, the British parties are more centralized, and their ideologies are more clearly defined. There are no primary elections; candidates for Parliament (the British equivalent of Congress) are chosen by the local party association. In the British parliamentary system, there are no elections for national office—only local elections for seats in parliament. Thus candidates do not need to appeal to a wide variety of incompatible groups in order to win election. As a result their campaigns tend to be simpler, shorter (taking an average of about three weeks), and much less expensive than those of their American counterparts.

Political campaigns in the United Kingdom are very strictly regulated by a series of laws enacted over the last century. According to law, the amount that candidates for Parliament may spend in their campaigns is determined by the number of registered voters in their district. Another important requirement is that every candidate must ap-

British prime minister and Conservative Party leader John Major campaigns in 1992. Short campaigns, spending limits, and free broadcast time are features of the British system.

point an official election agent, who is responsible for every financial transaction in the campaign and who may be criminally prosecuted for violation of the law. The election agent is the only person who is permitted to accept contributions or loans for the campaign and, aside from the candidate, is the only person permitted to authorize campaign expenditures. Because the candidate can be held legally responsible for the actions of the election agent, it is important for the candidate to select a trustworthy professional for the job. In 1870 a British court ruled that bribery by an agent could annul an election even though the candidate was not a party to it.

British law also requires full disclosure of election expenses. Within thirty-five days after the results of an election are announced, the election agent must file a minutely detailed report with the local election official. The report must contain the names of all contributors and the amounts they contributed, as well as bills and receipts for all expenditures. Both the candidate *and* the agent can be fined or sent to prison if they file a false report—even if only one of them knowingly made a false statement. Within ten days after receiving the report, the election official must publish it in two newspapers within the candidate's district. Candidates who fail to file a report are subject to a stiff fine for every day the report is late.

Because the limit on expenditures is high, few British politicians are tempted to evade the law. Temptation is also reduced by the fact that, unlike U.S. congressional candidates, they can take advantage of some free advertising. For example, candidates for Parliament are allowed to send one free mailing of election material to each of their constituents. Candidates are also given free television and radio time. This time is allotted fairly to all candidates and political parties. Indeed, it is against the law for a candidate to buy television time, and it is illegal for Britain's commercial television stations to accept political advertising. Other laws and policies are designed to ensure fairness and impartiality in political broadcasting.

The British regulations seem to work very well. Violations of the reporting laws and spending limits are usually minor. Besides, any politicians who spent an exorbitant amount of money on their campaigns would quickly incur the displeasure of the British public, which looks down on politicians who try to "buy" their way into office.

France. At first glance, the French political system bears little resemblance to our own. The French have many political parties, representing widely differing views, and often many candidates compete for one seat in the National Assembly. The parties are not required to reveal the sources or amounts of their funds. There are no legal limits on political contributions from individuals or organizations, and no regulations on the money received or spent by parties or candidates during political campaigns. Yet, despite the absence of regulations, few French candidates conduct expensive campaigns—largely because many of the costs that in the United States would be paid for by the candidate or the party are in France assumed by the government. For instance, the French government mails ballots and circulars, prepared by the candidates, to the voters. The government also reimburses candidates for some of the costs of preparing and printing these materials. Candidates in presidential and national elections also receive generous amounts of free television and radio time to get their messages across. According to law, media time is allocated fairly to all candidates—not just those of major parties. French law also requires that all candidates be given fair and equal treatment in information programs that deal with their statements and writings.

Sweden. Five political parties dominate the Swedish legislature. To fund its political campaigns, each of these parties collects dues from its members at the local level. The dues are assessed on a sliding scale based on the incomes of individual members. In addition, Swedish political parties receive state subsidies (based on the number of voters they represent), which they use to pay for publications and organization costs. Some of the revenue is given to the national party committees to pay for national campaigns, but no public disclosure of funds received or spent is required. The Swedes have no laws governing campaign finance. In the 1950s a committee appointed by the king decided that revealing the names of people or organizations who make contributions to a political party would be a violation of the principle of secrecy of elections. The committee also concluded that to exercise legislative or administrative control over campaign expenses would violate the country's democratic principles.

Although there are no legal restrictions on spending, campaigns in Sweden cost much less than in the United States—largely because all political parties and their candidates are given equal amounts of free time on Swedish television and radio to present their platforms and views. Swedish voters are given ample opportunity to learn about the issues and candidates through numerous debates and other political programs, which are presented with neutrality and objectivity. In fact, during the two months preceding a general election, nearly all broadcast time is devoted to the campaign. Clearly, Swedish broadcasting (which is jointly owned by the government and private interests) has done a thorough job of assuming the responsibility of informing citizens about candidates and issues.

Although regulations, restrictions, and practices of campaign finance vary in the countries discussed, all have some provision for their political parties to receive free broadcast time and all provide a government subsidy to the parties or to the candidates themselves. Campaigns in these countries take much less time than in our country, and violations of the laws carry stiff penalties. Of course, no law is worth much unless it is enforced, and enforcement of the laws in these countries has, from time to time, been lax. But their laws and practices, while different from our own, seem to effectively prevent the abuses that are widespread in the United States.

What might our own lawmakers learn from examining campaign finance practices in these and other foreign nations? Would any of these practices work in the United States? In the next chapter, we will examine some options for campaign finance reform in this country.

7 Can the System Be Reformed?

Increasing numbers of Americans are fed up with the government's apparent inability to deal with the nation's problems. Senate Majority Leader George J. Mitchell has said that the cynicism of the American public is due, in large part, to what he has termed "the overwhelming role of money in the election process." Celinda Lake, who conducted a poll in 1993 on campaign finance for the Center of New Democracy, an organization that favors spending limits, likewise concluded, "Voters are disgusted with the pernicious role of money in politics."[1] Stan Greenberg, a close adviser on President Clinton's 1992 election staff, noted: "The voters are still cynical and to keep voters believing change is possible we have to keep cleaning up the system."[2]

As long as politicians owe their allegiance to wealthy contributors and special-interest groups, and as long as their energies are devoted to rounding up funds for their political campaigns, they cannot tend to the business of the nation. A complete breakdown of the American political system could very well be the price the United States will

Clinton greets well-wishers during the 1992 campaign. As president, he proposed a package of campaign financing reforms.

pay unless the current system of campaign financing is overhauled. As political writer Elizabeth Drew stated, "Unless the problem of money is dealt with, it is unrealistic to expect the political process to improve in any other respect."[3]

Where Do We Start? Deciding how to reform existing federal campaign finance laws is not an easy task. An unlimited number of approaches could be taken, but our elected officials in Congress and the White House must reach agreement on whatever reforms are enacted. Setting clear goals may make their task easier. Following are some of the goals that have been suggested by political writers and elected officials.

- We must make sure that when our senators and representatives cast their votes in Congress, they do so on the basis of what is best for the country and for the people they represent. They will be free to do this only when they no longer have to worry about pleasing or offending people who can give or withhold a campaign contribution.
- The loyalties of our elected officials—from president on down—must be to the people who are entitled to vote for them. Politicians must be accountable to their constituents, rather than to some PAC or special-interest group, or to wealthy individuals located outside their districts or states.
- Ordinary people—even if they can't afford to contribute to political campaigns—must be made to feel that they matter just as much to their president, senators, and representatives as do the special-interest groups and big-money contributors.
- Qualified people, regardless of wealth, must be able to run for office. Instead of a system in which money determines who gets elected and who stays in office, we need a system that encourages the best and the brightest, promotes challenge and competition, and fosters the growth of new ideas.
- Challengers and incumbents must be freed from the incessant chase after money. If their minds

are not continually preoccupied with raising money, elected officials will be able to do the real work for which they were elected: finding solutions to the issues and problems that confront the nation.

- We must find ways to control and contain the continually spiraling costs of campaigning. The current system, in which the candidate who spends the most is most often the winner, forces candidates into the desperate chase after money. Their attempts to outspend one another have resulted in increasingly expensive campaigns.

- Campaigns should be financed only with money to which no strings are attached. The power exerted by special-interest groups, large corporations, and individual wealthy contributors must be kept in check or eliminated. Only when campaigns are paid for by contributions from people and groups who do not hope to receive financial benefits or other favors in return for their contributions, will our politicians be freed from their obsessions with fund-raising.

With these goals in mind, political writers, those who study our political processes, and a number of politicians themselves have offered up proposals for reform. Let's take a look at the pros and cons of some of their recommendations and suggestions.

Provide Public Financial Assistance. Under current law, candidates for president can receive federal matching funds. This money is donated by taxpayers who contribute to the fund by means of the $1 voluntary checkoff on their individual income tax returns. The tax checkoff plan could be extended to include not just the president but senators and representatives to Congress as well. Or public financial assistance could be provided by means of a federal "bank" account from which candidates could draw. The money might also be provided by an outright appropriation.

The amounts that candidates receive could be based on the number of votes cast in previous elections for those offices, or, in the case of senators and congressional representatives, on the number of registered voters in the nominee's state or district. Some people suggest that the amount the candidates would receive should be determined by whether they are major or minor candidates. Another suggestion is that the money would be paid not to the candidates themselves but directly to those who had rendered them goods or services. This would ensure that the subsidy was spent on the purposes for which it was intended.

Still another method is to have the government provide matching funds to congressional candidates who voluntarily limit their campaign spending to amounts that would be determined by law.[4] This was the approach taken by President Clinton in his May 1993 proposal. In that plan, congressional candidates who agreed to spending limits would receive vouchers to pay for television time, postage, and printing.

Proponents of public financing believe that it would encourage competition by guaranteeing challengers an adequate amount of funding.[5] Furthermore, public funding would remove a candidate's dependence on special-interest groups. According to political expert Richard Bolling, "The overwhelming majority of representatives and senators would more faithfully represent the interests of their constituents if they could afford to do so."[6] Public financing would enable elected officials to say "no" to PACs and special-interest groups.

Some say that although public financing may sound like a good idea, it has its drawbacks. How would government determine which candidate would get what sum of money? According to Frank J. Fahrenkopf, Jr., of the Republican National Committee, letting the government apportion the money is a bad idea: such a system would probably result in a perpetuation of the existing power distribution.[7] In addition, total public funding is not likely to appeal to voters, according to Fahrenkopf, because it has the appearance of forcing taxpayers to pay for the campaigns of incumbents.[8]

Political writer Larry Sabato proposed that instead of a spending ceiling, candidates should be given spending "floors."[9] Each candidate would receive a base amount, or "floor." This would ensure that each candidate would have a sufficient starting amount with which to wage a campaign. Spending "floors" would encourage more competition, whereas spending ceilings tend to benefit incumbents. Challengers usually have to spend more to wage a successful campaign against an incumbent and are, therefore, penalized by spending limits.

Set Spending Limits. Despite Sabato's argument above, many people feel that ceilings on the amount of money a candidate could spend would make elections more fair by further reducing the role of private funding in elections. Louisiana's Senator John Breaux, for one, said that a realistic ceiling for both Senate and House elections would eliminate the money chase and encourage elected officials to concentrate more on their jobs and less on fund-raising. Some people think that all politicians should be limited in the amount of money they can spend on their campaigns. These limits could be determined in a number of ways. The Clinton plan proposed a flat limit of $600,000 for House candidates, and variable limits for Senate candidates, depending on state population. However, campaign costs

"Sorry kid, but I can't be bought!"

Some people see public funding as the best way to curb the influence special interests have on Congress.

vary in different sections of the country. For example, a candidate in New York City must pay more for a television commercial than a candidate in, say, Tulsa, Oklahoma. The amounts each of these candidates would be entitled to spend could reflect such differences.

Limit PAC Contributions. Many political writers and citizen advocacy groups have urged limiting PAC contributions to the same level—$1,000 for each federal election—that is placed on contributions from individuals. As we have seen, the vast majority of federal candidates rely on PACs. Furthermore, the PAC system benefits incumbents, and many of the most powerful politicians are the recipients of the largest PAC contributions. Thus limiting PAC contributions would put incumbents and challengers on a more equal footing.[10]

Many politicians agree in principle that PAC money, because there is so much of it and because it is so unevenly distributed, has a powerful, corrosive influence on government. But these same politicians may be reluctant to enact laws that would curtail such a lucrative source of revenue. Although Bill Clinton had backed a $1,000 PAC limit during the 1992 presidential election campaign, his 1993 proposal did not include it. However, he did call for limits on the percentage of any candidate's funds that could be raised from PACs.

Limiting the amount of PAC money might actually have negative effects, some people argue.[11] Such a limitation might be considered unconstitutional, as a restriction of the First Amendment guarantee of free speech. Larry Sabato maintained that limiting PAC donations might, in the end, favor incumbents. A lid on PAC gifts would assure incumbents that their challengers will be able to raise less money to try to defeat them.

Reducing the amount of PAC money might also benefit wealthy candidates. At the present time, any candidate
can spend an unlimited amount of personal funds on his
own election. Restricting an opponent's fund base would
enhance a wealthy candidate's power.

Abolish PACs. Some critics maintain that the only way to
restore public confidence in the political process is to eliminate special-interest money altogether. A total ban on
PACs—and PAC money—would certainly be one of the
main steps toward achieving that end. But opponents of the
idea say that even if a law abolishing PACs were passed, it
would probably be ruled unconstitutional. Eliminating
PACs, according to Curtis Gans of the Committee for the
Study of the American Electorate, "raises real constitutional problems. Collective speech should be encouraged."[12] In *Buckley* v. *Valeo*, the Supreme Court ruled that
PACs are protected by the First Amendment right of association. Certainly, any bill containing a provision to outlaw
PACs would be subject to vigorous debate on the floor of
Congress, and passage of such a bill would probably be
very difficult. A ban on campaign contributions by lobbyists, which was part of the Clinton plan, was seen as facing
similar difficulties.

Ban Out-of-State Contributions. Another possible reform would ban contributions from individuals who are not
residents of the candidate's congressional district or state.
This would make the candidate accountable only to the
people of his or her district—not to Washington lobbyists,
not to outside interests, and not to PACs who, after all,
have little regard for the welfare of the candidate's constituents. Under this plan, challengers would finally be on a
level playing field with incumbents. Incumbents could no

longer rely on gifts from outside PACs or rich people. No longer could members of congressional health committees, for example, count on contributions from the American Medical Association or wealthy doctors around the country. Gifts from the medical profession would have to come from doctors within the candidate's own district.

Opponents of this idea say that such a ban would run counter to the doctrine, upheld by the Supreme Court in 1976, that in politics, money is speech. They contend that banning a contribution from a donor outside a candidate's district would be an infringement of that donor's right to free speech.

On the other hand, it can be argued that outside donations violate the basic principle of one person, one vote. The vote of, say, a New Jersey resident for senator can be diluted or negated by a substantial contribution from someone living in California. The power of the New Jerseyan's vote is further reduced when the senator takes precious time away from the job to travel to California to solicit contributions. Moreover, it is clear to most observers that gifts from nonresidents are seldom given without strings attached. Banning contributions from nonresidents—whether PACs or individuals—would be an important step toward cleaning up "improper influence and corruption."

Give Tax Credits. Another possible reform is to allow tax credits or deductions for individuals who make small contributions to political parties. One proposal would allow individuals to deduct 100 percent of contributions to political parties or to House and Senate candidates from the contributor's own state. Gifts to PACs would not be tax deductible. This would have the effect of strengthening political parties, while eliminating taxpayer funding going toward special interests. PACs would still be allowed to pursue their interests via unrestricted spending.

Regulate "Soft Money" Contributions. Current law places virtually no restrictions on how much money corporations or other big-money spenders can donate to state or national party committees for such activities as voter registration drives, phone banks, generic party advertising, grass-roots organizing, and other voter turnout and "party-building" operations. Just as PAC contributions may influence the actions and decisions of the politicians who receive them, so may large "soft money" contributions influence the platforms and activities of political parties. In fact, much of this money finds its way into the campaigns of politicians. In the last four months of the 1992 campaign alone, Democrats raised about $20 million in soft money, while the Republicans raised $13 million.[13] Although few politicians of either party publicly defend soft money, most of them would be loath to see a ban placed on these lucrative contributions. Nevertheless, outlawing or limiting soft money contributions would ensure a more democratic system; it would liberate parties from the influence of special interests and aid in returning control of the parties to the people. Some restrictions on soft money donations were proposed as part of the Clinton plan.

Change Election Broadcasts. According to Elizabeth Drew, the most effective way of lowering campaign costs would be to require broadcast stations to supply some free television time.[14] Television makes it possible for vast numbers of people to become acquainted with candidates and to witness firsthand the debate and discussion of political issues. However, because they often appear on news and discussion programs, well-known candidates and incumbents have distinct advantages over less-known challengers.[15] Free and equal time would make it possible for all candidates to air their views and result in a better-informed electorate.

At first glance, free time appears to be a good idea, but it presents many complicated problems. Would stations be required to provide free time to independent candidates and candidates of small, minority parties as well as candidates of major parties? Who would determine how much program time candidates should receive? Would the stations or the candidates control the format of such programs? Who would determine the times (daytime, prime time, late night) at which such programs would be aired? Would appearances by candidates on news and interview programs be counted as free time? Who would be responsible for maintaining ethical standards of truth and accuracy in these programs? How would the law be monitored and enforced?

One suggestion is to ban spot advertisements on television. Many federal candidates spend a large portion of their campaign funds on television commercials that run twenty, thirty, or sixty seconds in length. Although expensive, these short TV "bites" are often negative and of little informative value. At best, they attempt to sell candidates the way soft drinks, deodorants, and other consumer products are sold. At worst, they offer up half-truths or downright lies. Political columnist Tom Wicker agreed that these spots are superficial, expensive, and often vindictive, but believed that limiting these spots would be difficult if not unconstitutional.[16] Furthermore, how would television stations decide what is "permissible" advertising?

However, according to political writer Pat M. Holt, there is growing evidence that voters find this sort of cynical campaigning "boring, confusing, offensive, or all of the above."[17] Many political writers and media specialists believe the American public can be trusted to make accurate judgments about television messages. "As politically unsophisticated as voters are, they are extremely sophisticated as TV viewers," said one media manager.[18]

Another suggestion is to ban the airing of all political commercials at least one week before an election. A further idea is to provide free, equal airtime—in segments at least five minutes in length—to all federal candidates during the last week of a campaign. This would prevent well-financed candidates from drowning out their less affluent opponents with a media blitz in the critical final days of a campaign.

Regulate Independent Expenditures. The law currently defines an independent expenditure as

> *an expenditure by a person expressly advocating the election or defeat of a clearly identified candidate which is made without cooperation or consultation with any candidate, or any authorized committee or agent of such candidate, and which is not made in concert with, or at the request or suggestion of, any such candidate, or any authorized committee or agent of such candidate.*[19]

In *Buckley* v. *Valeo*, the Supreme Court struck down limits on independent expenditures, stating that they do "not presently appear to pose dangers of real or apparent corruption comparable to those identified with large campaign contributions."[20]

Nevertheless, some people have urged that such expenditures be regulated and that all independently sponsored political advertisements carry the name of the individual or group that paid for the ad. Many individually sponsored ads are directed against specific candidates. One proposal would let candidates who are attacked in these ads apply for public funds, in an amount equal to the sum spent on the ads targeting them, so that they could respond in ads of their own.

Other Suggestions for Reform. Another idea is to ban the use of the franking privilege by incumbents for twelve months preceding an election. Suspending this privilege, which allows incumbent politicians to send postage-free mail to their constituents, would put challengers on a more equal footing with incumbents.

This raises a sticky question. Elected officials need to contact their constituents about their opinions on issues. Totally banning the franking privilege would limit the amount of correspondence that officials could have with those who elected them. Perhaps officials could be allowed to use the franking privilege for opinion surveys and other publications that were not clearly election-related.

A final suggestion is to shorten the length of campaigns. Presidential campaigns are usually launched one year before the election is held. Senatorial and congressional campaigns also run for many months. If campaign time were cut in half, politicians would still have plenty of time to get their messages across to voters, while greatly reducing the costs of their campaigns.

Whatever our lawmakers choose to do—whether to enact some of the proposals outlined or to adapt ideas from other countries—it is clear that reforms are urgently needed. Voices in both the Republican and Democratic camps have declared that campaign finance reform is vitally necessary to the health of our political system. In his first major address to Congress in mid-February 1993, President Clinton stated, "We must begin again to make Government work for ordinary taxpayers, not simply for special interest groups."[21]

But will the reforms outlined above produce a better

system than the one we now have? How much will these reforms cost? Can we afford proposals such as public financing of elections?

Although change involves risk, it is hard to imagine a system less democratic than the present one. As we have seen, nearly 95 percent of PAC donations are given to incumbents, and incumbents spend more than challengers. Unreported "soft money" contributions pour additional millions into the coffers of entrenched politicians. Without question, money gives incumbents a clear advantage over challengers. Challengers who do not attract significant campaign contributions from special interests and wealthy individuals find it nearly impossible to get elected to federal office.

Public financing of all federal elections would put all candidates on a more equal footing. While they agree that the idea sounds good in principle, opponents of public financing say it would cost taxpayers too much. But just how much would it cost? According to the lobbying group Public Citizen, providing public funding at a 50 percent level would cost taxpayers $350 million every two years. One possible source for this money would be eliminating the tax deductions that businesses now take for lobbying expenses, which the White House has estimated would raise $978 million over five years.[22] That's a lot of money. But it is significantly less than Americans are already paying for the hidden cost of politics. Health-care costs offer one example.

Hidden Political Costs in Health Care. The spiraling costs of health care have heavily affected the American economy. The Commerce Department reported in January 1993 that health-care costs had climbed 12 percent in 1991, to a total of $838.5 billion. Medical bills now account for 14 percent of the entire U.S. economy, whereas in 1980 they accounted for just 9.4 percent.[23] Costs are so steep that many citizens can't afford health care at all. According to consumer advocate Ralph Nader, "At least 37 million Americans lack any type of health care coverage and as many as 65 million others are underinsured, meaning that they may not be able to afford a routine visit to their doctor."[24]

Various factors contribute to the high cost of health care, including overpriced pharmaceutical drugs (62 percent higher than in Canada), the medical profession's increasing reliance on high-tech equipment and procedures, the aging of the population, the rise in medical malpractice suits, and hospital costs. The insurance companies that offer health policies are also to blame. With more than 1,500 kinds of insurance forms in use, there is great waste and inefficiency.[25]

Why hasn't the United States improved its health-care system? One reason, according to Susan Estrich, who managed Michael Dukakis's 1988 presidential campaign, is campaign financing. *Common Cause* magazine agrees: "The real culprit [is] the medical industry money that keeps politicians in office. . . . The same insurance companies, doctors, hospitals and drug manufacturers that live off the . . . health care industry are battling comprehensive reform on Capitol Hill and in the White House."[26] Doctors, hospitals, business leaders, and insurance companies have poured millions of dollars in campaign money into both Democratic and Republican campaigns. In the first eighteen months of the 1992 election, health and insurance industries increased their campaign contributions 20 percent over the same period in the 1990 campaign. The top ten health PACs donated nearly $4.5 million to 1992 campaigns.[27] "It's a good illustration of the buying of the institution [Congress]," says Ellen Miller of the Center for Responsive Politics, a non-profit public policy study group. "It's not just one campaign contribution, or a glut of contributions before an important vote. It's years and years of being dependent on health care industry as a major source of campaign funds for enormous numbers of members. It means bills not introduced, hearings not held."[28]

However, one part of President Clinton's 1992 election campaign platform was a promise to reform the health-care system so that all Americans could afford basic medical care. His ideas for reform seemed certain to touch off furious debate, since almost any change would alienate one or more powerful health-care interest groups, such as doctors, hospitals, or insurance companies. According to John Rother, director of legislation and public policy for the American Association of Retired Persons (AARP), "Any reform will create millions of winners and millions of losers. Health care is the most emotional and personal of all public policy issues."[29]

Of course, health care is only one area affected by the flow of money into political campaigns. The costs of politics are hidden in the prices we pay at the supermarket, at the gas station, and other places. In fact, almost every issue facing society—from environmental pollution and education to crime and taxes, from homelessness and poverty to public transportation and national defense—is affected by these funds.

Because all these situations and many others are related to campaign financing, the hidden costs of the present system affect all of us. No one knows just how much these hidden costs amount to. But even the most conservative estimates place the hidden costs of health care alone at much more than the potential cost of public campaign financing.

Public financing of federal campaigns would solve many of the problems inherent in the current system. It would relieve politicians from the continual chase after money. If they were no longer indebted to special interests and wealthy contributors, they might pay more attention to the needs of ordinary people and do a better job of governing the nation. Public financing would force incumbents to be more accountable to their constituents, and it would offer challengers a better opportunity to bring fresh ideas before the public. Most of all, it would strengthen democracy and restore public confidence in the electoral process. And it would counter the ugly notion that our politicians and elections are for sale.

The question facing Congress and the administration is no longer whether we can afford to overhaul our campaign finance system, but whether we can afford *not* to. Whatever public financing of campaigns or other reforms may cost, they cannot cost nearly as much as the present system.

Some people believe that most of our legislators are so comfortable with the current system that they will never enact reforms. But as public awareness grows, our politicians may have little choice. When ordinary Americans realize that they are paying heavily for the current system of campaign financing through high food and dairy prices, overpriced medical care, exorbitant insurance rates, poor schools, inadequate public transportation, a weakened financial system, air and water pollution, and in a host of other ways, they will demand change.

An examination of the proposals outlined earlier in this chapter, and a look at the way other nations have dealt with campaign finance, will show many of the ways in which the current system can be improved. The most difficult task will be to convince our federal officials that the job can and must be done, if we are to preserve our government as the Founding Fathers intended—a government of the people, by the people, and for the people.

Notes

1. Jules Archer, *Winners and Losers: How Elections Work in America* (San Diego: Harcourt Brace Jovanovich, 1984), p. 7. Also quoted in Diana Reische, *Electing a U.S. President* (New York: Franklin Watts, 1992), p. 79.
2. "1991 Congressional Election Spending Jumps 52% to $678 Million" (press release by Federal Election Commission, March 4, 1993), p. 1.
3. Herbert Alexander, *Financing Politics* (Washington, D.C.: Congressional Quarterly Press, 1976) p. 10.
4. Elizabeth Drew, "Campaign Finance Reform Is Necessary," in David L. Bender and Bruno Leon, editors, *America's Elections* (St. Paul: Greenhaven Press, 1988), p. 55.
5. Quoted by Drew (1988), p. 58.

Chapter Two

1. Federal Election Commission press release, March 4, 1993, pp. 1–2.
2. Beth Donovan, "Constitutional Issues Frame Congressional Options" (*Congressional Quarterly*, February 27, 1993), p. 434.

3. Federal Election Commission press release, March 29, 1993.
4. Michael Wines, "Candidates for Congress Spent Record $678 Million, a 52% Jump" (*The New York Times*, National Edition, March 5, 1993). See also FEC press release, March 4, 1993, pp. 1–2.
5. *Ibid.*
6. *Ibid.*
7. Mark S. Hoffman, *The World Almanac and Book of Facts 1993* (New York: Pharos Books, 1992), p. 305.
8. Austin Ranney, *Channels of Power* (New York: Basic Books, 1983), p. 8. See also *Statistical Abstract of the United States, 1979* (Washington, D.C.: Bureau of the Census, 1979), Table 986, p. 587, and Edwin Diamond, *The Tin Kazoo* (Cambridge: MIT Press, 1975), p. 13.

Chapter Three

1. Alexander, *Financing Politics*, p. 22. Also quoted in Jules Abels, *The Degeneration of Our Presidential Election: A History and Analysis of an American Institution in Trouble* (New York: Macmillan, 1968), p. 83.
2. *Ibid.*, p. 24. Also see Eugene H. Roseboom, *A History of Presidential Elections* (New York: Macmillan, 1957), p. 25.
3. *Ibid.*, p. 28.
4. Donovan (February 27, 1993), p. 433.
5. *Ibid.*
6. *Ibid.*
7. Donovan, p. 432.
8. FEC press release, March 4, 1993, p. 2.

Chapter Four

1. FEC, p. 4.
2. Larry J. Sabato, *PAC Power* (New York: W. W. Norton & Company, 1985), p. 3. Sabato quotes Alexis de Tocqueville, *Democracy in America* (New York: Vintage Books, 1954), vol. 2, p. 114.

3. The League of Women Voters of California Education Fund, *Choosing the President 1992* (New York: Lyons & Burford, 1992), p. 40. The League credited this information to Herbert Alexander, *Financing the 1984 Election* (Lexington, Mass.: Lexington Books, 1983), p. 127, and Harold W. Stanley and Richard G. Niemi, *Vital Statistics on American Politics* (Washington, D.C.: Congressional Quarterly Press, 1990), p. 163.
4. Wines, "Candidates for Congress."
5. Sabato, p. xi. Sabato quotes Senator Lugar's statement in the U.S. Congress, Senate, Committee on Rules and Administration, *Hearing on the Federal Election Campaign Act of 1971, as Amended, and on Various Measures to Amend the Act: S. 85, S. 151, S. 732, S. 810, S. 1185, S. 1350, and S. 1684*, 98th Congress, 1st session, S HRG 98-588, May 17, 1983, p. 325.
6. From a direct-mail letter signed by Common Cause president Fred Wertheimer (undated, mailed in March 1993).
7. Elizabeth Drew, "Watch 'em Squirm" (*The New York Times Magazine*, March 14, 1993), p. 50.
8. Sabato, *PAC Power*, p. 65. Sabato quotes Nicholas Goldberg, "Shakedown in the Boardroom," *Washington Monthly 15* (December 1983), p. 14.
9. FEC press release, March 4, 1993, p. 33.
10. *Ibid.*, p. 49.
11. Figures reported by the FEC and quoted in the editorial "Real Political Reform Can't Wait" (*The New York Times*, February 21, 1993.)
12. Common Cause letter.
13. *Ibid.*
14. FEC press release, March 4, 1993, p. 2.
15. *The New York Times* editorial, February 21, 1993.

Chapter Five

1. Alexander, *Financing Politics*, p. 9.
2. Drew (1993), p. 33.
3. *Ibid.*
4. Sabato, p. 122.

5. *Ibid.*, p. xi.
6. *Ibid.*, p. 122.
7. Hoffman, *The World Almanac*, p. 714.
8. Martin Mayer, *The Greatest-Ever Bank Robbery: The Collapse of the Savings and Loan Industry* (New York: Macmillan, 1990), p. 1.

Chapter Six

1. Sabato, *PAC Power*, p. xii, quoting from a direct-mail letter signed by Common Cause president Fred Wertheimer (undated, mailed in March 1983).
2. Fred Wertheimer, "Political Action Committees Are Too Powerful," in *America's Elections*, edited by Bender and Leone, p. 66.
3. Quoted in Wertheimer, p. 69.
4. Quoted in Wertheimer, pp. 64–65.
5. Sabato, *PAC Power*, p. 170. See also Elizabeth Drew, "Politics and Money, Part I" (*The New Yorker*, December 6, 1982), p. 147.
6. Sabato, p. 185.

Chapter Seven

1. Donovan (February 27, 1993), p. 431.
2. Drew (1993), p. 50.
3. Drew (quoted in Bender and Leone), p. 54.
4. Donovan (February 27, 1993), pp. 434–435.
5. Charles McC. Mathias, Jr., "Taxpayers Should Finance Political Campaigns" in *America's Elections*, edited by Bender and Leon, p. 84.
6. *Ibid.*, p. 79.
7. Frank J. Fahrenkopf, Jr., "Taxpayers Should Not Finance Political Campaigns," in *America's Elections*, p. 86.
8. *Ibid.*, p. 85.
9. Sabato, *PAC Power*, p. 179.
10. Wertheimer, "Political Action Committees," p. 66.
11. Sabato, pp. 173–174.
12. Donovan (February 27, 1993), p. 436.

13. Drew (1993), p. 33.
14. *Ibid.*, p. 74.
15. Doris A. Graber, *Mass Media and American Politics* (Washington, D.C.: Congressional Quarterly Press, 1989), p. 204.
16. Tom Wicker and Pat M. Holt, "Campaign Advertising Is Harmful," in *America's Elections*, edited by Bender and Leone, pp. 117–118.
17. *Ibid.*, p. 120.
18. Edwin Diamond and Stephen Bates, "Campaign Advertising Is Not Harmful," in *America's Elections*, p. 124.
19. Mathias, in *America's Elections*, p. 80.
20. *Ibid.*, p. 79.
21. Drew (1993), p. 33.
22. Beth Donovan, "Clinton Readies Proposals" (*Congressional Quarterly*, March 20, 1993), p. 646.
23. Janice Castro, "Paging Dr. Clinton" (*Time*, January 18, 1993), p. 24.
24. Quoted in *The Washington Spectator*, Vol. 18, No. 9, 1992, p. 1.
25. Castro, p. 26.
26. Quoted in *The Washington Spectator*, Vol. 18, No. 9, 1992, pp. 2–3.
27. Figures reported by Citizen Action and published in *The New York Times* (November 15, 1992).
28. *New Orleans Times Picayune*, January 2, 1992.
29. Castro, p. 24.

For Further Information

Recommended Reading

Alexander, Herbert E. *Financing Politics*. Washington, D.C.: Congressional Quarterly Press, 1984.

Alexander, Herbert E., and Brian A. Haggerty. *Financing the 1984 Election*. Lexington, Ky.: Lexington Books, 1987.

Archer, Jules. *Winners and Losers: How Elections Work in America*. San Diego: Harcourt Brace Jovanovich, 1984.

Barone, Michael, and Grant Ujifusa. *The Almanac of American Politics 1992*. Washington, D.C.: National Journal, 1991.

Drew, Elizabeth. *Politics and Money: The New Road to Corruption*. New York: Macmillan, 1983.

Edsall, Thomas Byrne. *Power and Money: Writing About Politics, 1971–1987*. New York: W.W. Norton & Co., 1988.

Graber, Doris A. *Mass Media and American Politics*. Washington, D.C.: Congressional Quarterly Press, 1989.

Guzzetta, S. J. *The Campaign Manual: A Definitive Study of the Modern Political Campaign Process*. Alexandria, Va.: Campaign Publishing Co., Inc., 1981.

Jackson, Brooks. *Honest Graft: Big Money and the American Political Process.* New York: Alfred A. Knopf, Inc., 1988.

League of Women Voters of California Education Fund. *Choosing the President 1992.* New York: Lyons & Burford, 1992.

Mayer, Martin. *The Greatest-Ever Bank Robbery: The Collapse of the Savings and Loan Industry.* New York: Charles Scribner's Sons, 1990.

Modl, Thomas, editor. *America's Elections: Opposing Viewpoints.* San Diego: Greenhaven Press, 1988.

Raber, Thomas R. *Presidential Campaign.* Minneapolis: Lerner Publications Company, 1988.

Ranney, Austin. *Channels of Power.* New York: Basic Books, 1983.

Reische, Diana. *Electing a U.S. President.* New York: Franklin Watts, 1992.

Sabato, Larry J. *PAC Power.* New York: W. W. Norton & Co., 1985.

Salmore, Stephen A. and Barbara. *Candidates, Parties, and Campaigns.* Washington, D.C.: Congressional Quarterly Press, 1985.

Stern, Philip M. *The Best Congress Money Can Buy.* New York: Pantheon Books, 1988.

Organizations to Contact

American Enterprise Institute
for Public Policy Research (AEI)
1150 17th Street N.W., Washington, D.C. 20036
(202) 862-5800

AEI has published books and pamphlets on topics including campaign finance and political parties. After every election, the institute publishes studies on the results.

Cato Institute
224 Second Street S.E.,Washington, D.C. 20003
(202) 546-0200

The Cato Institute believes that government should be limited so that individual liberty may be respected. Therefore, it is opposed to federal regulation of election campaigns. It publishes *Policy Analyses*, a series of position papers covering topics such as campaign finance and political action committees.

Citizens' Research Foundation
USC Research Annex
3716 South Hope Street, Los Angeles, CA 90007
(213) 743-5211 FAX (213) 743-3130

The foundation collects data on campaign contributions and studies election trends and results, which it publishes in pamphlets and books.

Common Cause
2030 M Street N.W., Washington, D.C. 20036
(202) 833-1200

Common Cause is a nonprofit public-interest organization with more than 250,000 members. It works toward reforms in campaign financing and political action committees. It publishes articles on campaign finance in *Common Cause Magazine* as well as ongoing campaign finance studies.

The Federal Election Commission
999 E Street N.W.,Washington, D.C. 20463
(202) 219-4155 Toll Free (800) 424-9530

The commission, which consists of six members appointed by the president and confirmed by the Senate, certifies the federal matching funds given to qualifying presidential candidates. Its press office reports on election results.

The League of Women Voters Education Fund
1730 M Street N.W.,Washington, D.C. 20036
(202) 429-1965

A part of the League of Women Voters, the fund promotes education on election issues and publishes pamphlets. The league is a volunteer organization of women and men dedicated to working toward political responsibility. Most communities have a branch of the league.

Public Affairs Council
1019 19th Street N.W.,Washington, D.C. 20036
(202) 872-1790

The council is a professional association of executives from corporations and other organizations. It publishes newsletters and reports on campaign finance and political action committees.

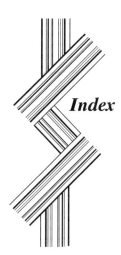

Index

Page numbers in *italics* refer to illustrations.